VIRGINIA MAYO

THE BEST YEARS
OF MY LIFE

as told to LC Van Savage

www.beachhousebooks.com

BeachHouse Books

Chesterfield Missouri

Copyright

Graphics Credits:

The original painting of Virginia Mayo on the cover is by David Fairrington, reproduced with permission.
 e-mail: fairrington@mindspring.com See more of his work on the web:
http://fairrington.home.mindspring.com

thanks to Ed G. Lousararian and Marvin Paige for helping us locate photographs. Most of the movie stills are reprinted with permission from Time -Warner, as noted. We have done our best to identify sources, ownership's and permissions . Please let us know of any errors or omissions and they will be corrected

ISBN 1-888725-53-2

Publication date February, 2002
First Printing, February, 2002

Library of Congress Cataloging-in-Publication Data
Mayo, Virginia, 1920-
 Virginia Mayo : the best years of my life / as told to LC van Savage.
   p. cm.
 ISBN 1-888725-53-2 (alk. paper)
 1. Mayo, Virginia, 1920- 2. Motion picture actors and actresses--United States--Biography. I. Van Savage, LC, 1938- II. Title.
 PN2287.M544 A3 2001
 791.43'028'092--dc21   2001003364

www.beachhousebooks.com

BeachHouse
Books

an Imprint of
Science & Humanities Press

PO Box 7151
Chesterfield, MO 63006-7151
(636) 394-4950
sciencehumanitiespress.com

Prologue

My friendship with Virginia Mayo goes a long way back, well over seventy-two years. We share almost a lifetime of memories.

We met at Benton School in St. Louis, Missouri, in the second—or was it the third grade?--and from that time on, we have always been close. I recall how we would escape the summer heat by drawing pictures and playing games in our cool basements. We loved to roller skate, to take walks and go swimming in the Sherman Park pool. I still have a memory of Virginia standing before the radio in her home, mouthing words and performing. What a ham! Occasionally on Fridays, if we had 15 cents, we walked across the street to Mr. Tucker's Restaurant and bought our lunch; fish, potatoes and coleslaw. A real treat!

I also recall a Bridge Club we formed with three friends; Mary Jane Jennings, Marguerite Gay and Elizabeth Thornley. We felt very mature, though we were not very good at playing cards. But we surely did love the dessert each "hostess" made when it was her turn.

Finally we all graduated and eventually, Virginia moved, necessitating her attending a different school. She enrolled at Soldan High School while I attended Beaumont High. But though we were separated, we always kept in touch. Virginia has been a very dear and loyal friend.

When Virginia moved West and began her movie career, I visited the home she shared out there with her mother, a wonderful, sweet lady. I recall going to the studio for the day to watch Virginia make a movie with Bob Hope.

In July, 1947, when Virginia and Michael O'Shea were married, I was her only attendant. In September, 1947, she was my only attendant at my marriage to Gordon Kirschbaum. For years we exchanged dinner invitations. Michael and Virginia were godparents to our son Kim. It was a joy to watch their daughter Mary Catherine grow up in such a happy home. There are no words to express the loss our family felt when Michael died. He was such a warm-hearted, humorous, generous person, and a loving husband and father.

Since then, though years have passed, nothing has changed. Virginia and I are still, as she says, "best buddies." I count myself lucky to know her.

Audrey Kirschbaum

DEDICATION

I want to dedicate this book to several people who are important in my life. First and always, my beloved daughter Mary. She has been my best friend since the moment she was born. We share a full and happy life.

To Mary's dear husband Kent; thanks for keeping me supplied with candy and cream soda. To my three adored grandsons, Lucas, Evan and Dillon, my able helpers and VCR technicians.

And lastly, I dedicate this book to my good and loving parents who gave me a happy childhood, who taught me the importance of hard work and commitment, who always told me to follow my dreams and were proud of me when I did.

ACKNOWLEDGMENTS:

I wish to acknowledge my grandmother, Ella Jones of St. Louis, Missouri, who greatly influenced my life. She was a member in good standing of the Daughters of the American Revolution, a worthy organization of which I am a proud member of long standing.

And also, Dorothy Roodman of St. Louis, my wonderful dancing pal Jane Pearson of Scottsdale, four times in the Muny. Jody Taylor who played in several plays with me, a wonderful actress. Laura Wagner of Long Island, New York, who did much research on my behalf, and Randal Malone who gives me endless companionship and laughter.

I wish to thank Lyn Hall who has always worked hard on my behalf. I could not handle the large amount of mail that comes to me without her unending help.

VIRGINIA MAYO

THE BEST YEARS
OF MY LIFE

CHAPTER 1

It was over. Finished. I'd been making successful movies for three major film studios since I first began my film career in the late nineteen forties. Five of the last fifteen years of my movie making were with Sam Goldwyn and RKO Pictures. And now, more than thirty years after the start of my long and varied movie career in comic, dramatic and musical films, it was abruptly finished. Done. I suddenly discovered I was simply to be gone, quietly to disappear after so many years, like a bubble popping and vanishing into thin air.

I tried to pretend it didn't hurt, but it did. I tried to pretend I didn't care, but I did. It's never been my style to let my emotions get the better of me, to give in to pain, sadness or regret, so I wasn't about to start then. But I would not be telling the truth if I said this final moment didn't cause me anguish.

So I cannot really say that this ending of such an important part of my life had no effect on me. Sure it did. But my contract was up. Ended. I felt as if I'd been cut adrift at sea and that no one in this business I'd come to love either noticed I was leaving or cared in the least what might happen to me. No one even looked up as I walked out of those doors and walked to my car. No one waved. No one said thank you. No party. No cake. No lunch. No one even said goodbye. I just simply got into my car and drove home.

I'd made millions for those studios and had never once caused any trouble. Never late. No scandal. No endless affairs with my leading men. I showed up on time every day, had my lines learned, and did exactly what was expected of me. I played by the rules, stayed out of trouble, and never once embarrassed the Hollywood studio heads.

It was my beloved parents in St. Louis, Missouri, who taught me to have this solid work ethic. Nine years after I was born, the Great Depression hit, so I, like millions of others, did what was expected of me: I helped the family out financially, and I continued to do so until my parents died. Part of all my salaries went to them, starting in the very early years of my career when I was in vaudeville, and even before when I danced at the Muny

Opera in St. Louis. Always. It was what was expected of me, and I did it without giving it a single thought. There was no room for debate. The money was needed, I had it, so I gave some of it to them.

I was taught to honor work and be grateful for it, taught quite early in life that if someone were going to pay me a salary, then I had certain obligations to them. With regard to my movie work, I can today look into the mirror and say I met those obligations. All of them.

I remember hearing about Clark Gable's also being abruptly dumped out the door when his contract was up. He'd been a top box-office draw for as many years as I had, and more. He was "The King of Hollywood," but on the day his contract was up, he too just got into his car and went home. No party. No thank you's. He drove through the gates and out onto the highway. King Clark was as nothing. Considering the pleasure and fun he'd given the movie-going world, that was a crime, but no one cared then, and no one cares now. He was gone, and so was his memory. Clark died a short time later.

The Sultan of Morocco once sent a letter to the studio heads stating that I was "tangible proof of the existence of God." Well, so much for that. The proof of the existence of God was quite suddenly a has-been and proof of nothing at all.

But I wasn't quite finished then. And I'm sure not now!

My name is Virginia Mayo. It wasn't always. When my mother, Martha Henrietta Rautenstrauch Jones gave birth to me on November 30, 1920, it was in a hurry. She was at the movies and had to run home to have me, so it might be said that I wanted to be in the movies from even before I was born! We never made it to the hospital. I was born at home in my parents' apartment. They named me Virginia Clara Jones. I kept that name for nearly twenty years.

I have an ancestry I'm proud of. My last name was Jones, and my father's family came from Wales. The family moved to Canada, I'm not exactly sure when or even why, and in time moved to and settled in Missouri where I was born.

I say with great pride that I'm a member in good standing of the Daughters of the American Revolution, the St. Louis branch. Private Joseph Fenton and Captain Piggott were our relatives and both fought bravely in the American Revolution. Private Fenton was in Company D of the Missouri Infantry. Captain Piggott fought with General George Washington at Brandywine. When he finished with the war, he moved west and settled in Illinois. By building the first courthouse and founding the first ferryboat

2

system to go across the Mississippi River separating Missouri and Illinois, he became a very important man. I am extremely proud to be related to these noble men.

My paternal grandmother Helen Jones was in the DAR and always wore all those sashes and ribbons with pride. All my female family relatives joined that auspicious group of women. I'm unfortunately unable to go to meetings, but I do keep up my dues and still belong to the St. Louis chapter.

Edie Adams. Remember her? She was married to that very funny comedian Ernie Kovacs and was also a member of the DAR. Sometimes she and I would plan on going to Washington, D. C. to present ourselves to the DAR members there. It was our wish to show them that yes, even actresses can belong to important organizations such as the DAR. We thought it would be a great boost for our careers, too. But we never got around to it, I'm sorry to say.

Over the years people have frequently asked me if something special was noticed about me when I was young. Did I have a certain "spark"? Stand out in a crowd? Was I a beautiful child? No. No one ever said I was cute or pretty. I was really kind of skinny. Beautiful curly light blonde hair, green eyes, yes. But I never had that "look" until I hit about seventeen. Then I got it! Pretty as a child? Never, at least not in those middle years from cute toddler to pretty teenager.

And on top of that, I was also very sickly! I had every disease known back then, and at age five even caught Diphtheria and Scarlet Fever at the same time! Can you imagine that? People were constantly dying from one or the other, and I had both. I think that's what Helen Keller had as a baby, wasn't it? The diseases that took away her sight and hearing and ability to speak? I was extremely lucky to come out of that. My poor mother and father were worried and frightened. I know they were preparing themselves for my inevitable death.

My dear mother stayed home with me every single minute of every long day of that illness, taking such good care of me. I loved her for that. And I still do. What a sacrifice! She showed me her love by doing that.

I remember that during this illness my hair started to fall out. The doctor told my mother to have my head completely shaved or my hair would not grow back. Well, she did it, very reluctantly and over my loud protests. I suddenly found myself totally bald. But only for a while. Eventually it began to grow back. It was (and still is,) really nice hair.

But I survived. And my brother Lea? He never got anything. Never. His name was Lea Lake Jones. Lea is a family name, pronounced "Lee." He was a nice guy and even though we were at opposite ends of the country, I miss him. He was an administrative assistant in a large and very profitable rock crushing business in Manassas, Virginia. Like me, Lea was matter-of-fact and not easily excited. Of good Midwestern stock! We were close and kept in touch with each other until he died.

CHAPTER 2

She was my father's sister. Her name was Aunt Alice, Alice Jones Wientge. I wondered sometimes when I was small if she'd ever wanted to be a singer and dancer in show business. I never asked her that, but what I do know is that it was she who helped make all my dreams come true. It was she who began my career by teaching me to be poised, to speak clearly. She taught phonetics. It was she who gave me drama lessons, elocution lessons. It was she who taught me to dance. She called her school "Aunt Alice's School of Dramatic Expression."

I can still hear Aunt Alice making us go over and over the vowels, to say them properly. Seventy five years later I can still recite "Round the rough and rugged rocks the ragged rascals rudely ran!" I took part in many skits and remember them clearly. I even remember all the beautiful, creative costumes Aunt Alice and our families made for us, and we made ourselves. By the time I was seven, I was completely comfortable on the stage. I loved being there. Every single second of it. Well, except for maybe one small incident.

Marguerite Gay, who was my partner back then, was very talented. She too was skinny and about as tall as I was. We were a great duo act. We enjoyed our show-business life even though we were so young. One performance when I was dancing and doing an act with Marguerite, I was playing the boy's role. We were singing a tune called "Hanging On The Garden Gate." I desperately had to visit the bathroom but felt ashamed to ask if I could go because we were just about to go on stage! And so, you guessed it. It just happened. I thoroughly wet my pants. Oh, the embarrassment!

It was awful. I had to confess to Aunt Alice because I could hardly go on stage with a huge stain on my britches. She was a kind woman and understood kids. Thinking quickly, she told us to put on our Scottish kilts. So, we immediately did our Scotch routine. The day was saved, and so was my dignity. The show went on!

Aunt Alice taught me to exploit my natural talent. Once my instruction from her began, there was nothing for me but to perform. For the rest of my life!

I remember sometimes she'd ask me to take over for her, to teach the kids while she went off to do something else, and I knew then that being a teacher was something I would never want to do! Boring! But I surely loved learning and being taught. If she can hear me, I want to say, "Thank you, Aunt Alice." Aunt Alice was the beginning of my professional life, a life that has allowed me to meet people and go places the good folks of St. Louis, Missouri had probably never even dreamed of.

Aunt Alice's teachings cut severely into my academic schooling, and all those absences left me with large chunks of missed education. I could not write a decent composition and confess here that I used to ask my father to write them for me. I'd get great grades because of him. My father was a wonderful writer. He wrote newspaper stories for the St. Louis Globe Democrat for many years. I was so proud of him.

To my endless regret, I never learned arithmetic either. In this case, I'd ask my brother to do my arithmetic homework. And I'd get good grades in that too. Luckily I'd even get out of having to take tests because I'd be off performing somewhere. Oh my, I do have a past! It sounds funny now, but I really still feel the absence of those basic teachings, sixty-five years later. I still can't do any of those subjects awfully well.

I did, oddly enough, excel in my high school, Soldan, largely because there I was able to take courses relating to the arts. I didn't have to leave school so often during my high school years to do shows around town, but I was expected to perform on stage, mostly dancing, and to stage and direct shows. These activities gave me credits toward graduation.

I took a lot of art classes in high school too, still paint today and I'm a pretty good painter. For a short time I did consider becoming a serious painter as a career. But then, no. I knew for certain it had to be show business for me; then, now, always. Anyway, I did graduate from highschool.

Aunt Alice didn't teach me all my dancing. She brought in a marvelous "tapper" named Cliff Dillon, who gave me invaluable lessons in tap. In St. Louis back then any kids could go to a place called Sherman Park Funding Dance School, where dance teachers, sponsored by the city, would come in and teach, for free!

Even ballet. I learned to do "toe work" and later on in my career, there's a very famous full length picture of me on my toes, wearing ballet

6

slippers. I didn't do much ballet throughout my career, but I knew how to do it! It was an incredible discipline and I wouldn't have missed it. I wasn't all that good at it, but I did learn it. It's extremely difficult, and I very much admire people dedicated to the ballet.

This was the Depression, don't forget, and these things were offered to anyone who wanted the training at no charge. I don't know how these teachers got paid, or even if they did, but they taught us well. Aunt Alice would bring in wonderful tap dance teachers too, and I got really good at that. I even learned to do dance numbers on stairs! The teachers would bring in a set of portable steps and we'd dance on them. I never fell once and never broke anything. They taught me to fall properly anyway, and I learned how to never get hurt if I did fall. Up and down those stairs we'd dance and tap, and we'd even do dance numbers on top. This was an invaluable experience for me. I tapped in a lot of films, and I was good at it because of the basics I learned at Sherman Park.

I've been asked often over the years when it was I first realized I wanted to go into show business, and I can honestly say there was never a time when I actually had this big Epiphany or something. It was just simply always that way with me. It was my dream from the time I was able to dream. I absolutely cannot remember ever giving consideration to any other kind of life. It was the only thing about myself and my future I thoroughly, completely understood, from the very beginning of me, Virginia Clara Jones of St. Louis, Missouri.

Because of Aunt Alice's hard work with me, and because of my own continued hard work, I was privileged to be part of a unique piece of American history--—the Golden Years of Hollywood, as they were called. Alas, they have ended, as all eras must. I miss those days but do not regret that where I am and what I am today is far removed from those glittering glory days. They are part of what made me. They were my dreams come true. I am honored to have been a part of a form of entertainment that gave much joy to many. Those movies and the people who created them were the rock foundation of the movie industry today. Those days can never return, but thanks to the preservation of those magical, wondrous films, they will never be forgotten.

I well remember Lea's once having to join Aunt Alice and her troops, and being assigned a role in a recital. Well, his cue came and came, and nothing happened. Aunt Alice went searching for him, and found him, sound asleep back stage. We got the message. That was the end of Lea's showbiz career. He had no aptitude at all. My mother pulled him out of there instantly.

All of Aunt Alice's students were expected to do whatever she taught us. Part of my early training with her was for me and the other kids in her school to go out into St. Louis to perform for many of her customers who frequently wanted free entertainment. We also successfully put on skits for the Masons and the Shriners and other service organizations, and we were always a big hit. We kids could do anything!

Every year Aunt Alice would have us put on a huge recital. It was fabulous training for what was to come for me later on. But back then, as I was entering my teen years, I'd suddenly become very frightened at the thought of those recitals, even though I'd been doing lots of shows all year long. But she made us all go through it, and I was able to overcome my stage fright because of Aunt Alice's patient training and discipline. Can you imagine having stage fright and wanting to go into show business? There's no place for it. If you commit to a show, you just do it and you simply do not give in to the butterflies. Ever.

I well remember a most interesting event when I was a child of about seven. Charles Lindbergh had made his famous flight to France, the first to fly the Atlantic in one nonstop flight. Of course, he began his journey from St. Louis where he was sponsored by businessmen.

We were all so proud of him and I can remember going to see his plane "The Spirit of St. Louis" when it was on display at the art museum. I could even touch it. I will never forget how the glittery design on the fuselage shown out, reflecting on my hand as I reached to touch it.

Now the plane hangs high at the Smithsonian, but I guess that's because people were tearing pieces from it for souvenirs. What's the matter with people?? Why do they have to do that?

But anyway, the day before this marvelous event, our teacher said that we'd all have to be on the levee by noon the next day because Lindbergh would be flying over St. Louis. We were going to see him! Our teachers told us his plane came on a boat from Paris to New York City, and he'd be flying it back to St. Louis the very next day. They promised he'd be flying low for all of us so we would be able to greet him!

Sure enough, while we stood right there on the banks of the Mississippi River, Lucky Lindy flew by in The Spirit of St. Louis. He brought the plane down low enough so that we really could see it well and even see him in the cockpit. There he was, grinning down at us and smiling his famous, boyish grin. We kids waved madly! It was a thrill then and a thrill now when I remember that morning. I've never forgotten it. Lindbergh was my hero. I used to dream about him all the time and would wish he'd be my boyfriend.

8

Later on, When Lindbergh began his airmail flights, my father wrote a letter to someone and it was carried on one of his planes, and I still have that very letter!

Imagine! I got to see that wonderful piece of American history on that day in 1927, and I can remember it as clearly as if it happened yesterday. I still can't get over it! That wonderful man, smiling and waving at us kids on the levee. I adored him. I will always be so grateful that I wasn't out doing a performance that day.

Back when I was a child in St. Louis, they had something called the St. Louis Municipal Opera, or "The Muny." It still exists today and is still famous. Everyone in Missouri, and especially in St. Louis, who performed or dreamed of going into showbusiness first dreamt of being on that fabulous stage. And this was my passion as a kid, to go to performances and eventually become a performer there. And for all the good things my parents were to me, I still recall the pain it caused me when they simply would not take me to the shows at "The Muny."

The Muny to me was what Carnegie Hall and the Roxy Theater and Radio City Music Hall and the Palladium were to performers in New York City. It was the tops, the pinnacle, and the most coveted place to be in St. Louis.

Maybe they thought I wouldn't appreciate it, that after all I was only a kid. (A kid who was putting on endless shows with Aunt Alice's School of Dramatic Expression.) Or maybe they just needed an occasional night out alone. Oh, how I yearned go to The Muny. Eventually I'd get there to watch the shows and finally to perform on that great outdoor stage. Years later in 1955, when I was 35 years old, I went back there for a lot of reasons, one of them being a "photo shoot." I sat there with all the empty seats behind me and the memories flooded back to me. I remembered dancing on that old stage outside in the wonderfully warm, beautiful Missouri weather.

I remembered the applause, the other girls I danced with. That picture shows me looking off into the distance, but I was not acting in that shot---I was remembering. The Muny Opera was the beginning, really, of my show business career. Aunt Alice trained me, but the Muny launched me.

I remember thinking, as I sat there for that photo shot, that when I finally got to dance on that marvelous old stage, I'd arrived and that nothing, absolutely nothing could get any better in my life than that! I'd achieved absolutely everything in life—I was dancing on the Muny stage! I would never want or need one more thing out of life. I know very well that had it not been for the Muny, nothing else would have happened for me. It was a glorious experience.

But before I had that experience, when my dear brother Lea and I got into our teens, we'd walk there. It was a very long walk, but worth every step. We'd get into the free seats and bring sandwiches so we wouldn't get hungry during the performances. As we'd watch those marvelous musical comedies and operettas at the Muny, I would sit there transported. It was where I belonged, and I knew it.

Not so Lea. He liked the shows, I guess, but Lea has never for an instant had the same sort of tug and yearning I had for show business. Not a glimmer! We'd see shows like the famous Show Boat and other grand and famous operettas, and I would sit there loving them, drinking them in, getting lost in them. But not Lea. For me, those shows were the livin' end! For him, they were just the end.

I clearly remember a leading performer at the Muny named Audrey Christie who just grabbed hold of my heart when she danced and sang. I thank her today for opening up my soul to this wonderful world of music and dance. Like Aunt Alice, she inspired me greatly. I was meant for a life in show business.

And then there were my poor friends! When I was a kid and we'd all run outside to play, there would be none of the usual hide-and-go-seek or kick the can, jacks, tag, roller skating jump rope or building tree houses. At least, not for me. No way! I'd gather everyone around me and shout, "Let's play show!" And I'd yell it louder and louder and begin assigning various kids to various roles, and eventually, they'd let me boss them into a "show," and I'd be able to "perform" right there in my own yard. Oh, I was so bossy! But it didn't always work, mind you. The kids didn't have the same passion for show business I had. As a matter of fact, they didn't care about it at all. I just couldn't understand that kind of thinking, and still can't! I'm kidding, but in fact I just know those kids weren't born to be in it the way I had been. I truly believe that. It was predestined, and I know and believe it. I was meant for a life in show business from the moment of my conception.

My father, Luke Ward Jones, was a man of note in St. Louis. Amongst other things, he was president of the PTA, and was for twenty-one years a very well known writer for the St. Louis Globe Democrat, I was never expected to make up for my lost school time, due to my going about St. Louis to put on performances with Aunt Alice's group, and to this day I sorely regret that, because I didn't learn all the things I should have in grammar school.

But alas, my dear father lost his job at the paper because of the Depression, and that good man worked at any number of jobs in the following years so that we could eat and have that roof over our heads. Oh

10

how hard he worked for us. What a terrible, terrible time it was indeed. No one had a job. My mother didn't work because she had to stay home with us. We even had to give up the sweet little house we lived in on top of a hill. I remember we had to move in with my Aunt Adelaide. Her husband had left her so I expect she was grateful to have a man around the house again. But oh, it was crowded because my grandparents had to move in too, along with the four of us. The Great Depression was such a terrible time. No one can know unless they've lived through it.

My beloved brother Lea did what I consider to be the most noble of things back then. We all were expected to contribute to the household money pot, and I recall my dear brother being offered a job in New York City with Liggett and Meyers Tobacco Company. We were fortunate enough to have a rich relative who could offer this to him. Lea would have to quit high -school and accept this job because like all families back then, we were desperate to have the money. But Lea was a sweet and good young man (and he stayed that way always) and he agreed to do it although he didn't want to stop his schooling. So off he went. The job would be in St. Louis although their headquarters were in New York City.

I don't know what his position was, but I do know he was diligent and worked very hard for L&M, but his conscience began to bother him. A lot. In time he had to quit that job even though he knew how much the money was needed, because he knew that cigarettes were bad for people and he just could not, in good conscience, keep on working for a company he thought was damaging people's health. He was way before his time. But that was typical of my dear brother. My family supported his decision, and he came back home and went to night school to get his diploma, to his credit. He was a very admirable person, was Lea. I love him very much and I miss him.

Lea and I both gave our paychecks, or part of our paychecks to our family for years and years.

I learned much from my family and my father back then, about the importance of hard work, the importance of a dependable salary. These lessons would stand me in good stead for the rest of my life.

CHAPTER 3

It was 1937, and to my family's delight I graduated from high school with honors, thanks to all those shows I produced for the school, and thanks to my artistic abilities with oil and canvas. I was seventeen, full of life and plans, and definitely on my way. There would be no stopping Virginia Clara Jones of St. Louis, Missouri!

My first plan was to get a part at The Muny. In 1936, the year before I graduated from highschool, I had auditioned, bursting with confidence.

But, I was rejected! Impossible! After all Aunt Alice's training! Well, I had been expected to do the steps for a dance routine they showed me, and I didn't do so well. I just didn't cut it! But I learned quickly that if you are convinced that show business is to be your career, you take the blows, get up and audition again. This is exactly what I did a year later.

But this time, I did a couple of other things to make certain I'd win the next audition. I made a costume. It was short and I made it on my own sewing machine. It was turquoise satin, and cut to my hip with a row of tiny pleats in a very short skirt. I learned those steps, learned how to deliver them, showed my legs and did the job. I won! I was accepted for a role in my beloved, coveted St. Louis Municipal Opera Company. I would perform and dance there outdoors at night for a full summer. Ten thousand seats! Huge trees on both sides of the stage. One show seven days a week; doing one, learning the next show as we performed. I'd always immediately and vigorously volunteer for any speaking parts, and I'd get them too. My parents were so proud. My mother told me she could always spot me immediately, even if I was buried in the big chorus of thirty girls and ten boys. Talk about seventh heaven! I'd made the Muny Opera! Aunt Alice, I really owe you!

I spent that summer working in the Muny Opera in a state of complete joy, but winter even comes to St. Louis, Missouri, and I had to think of moving on. Don't forget – The Muny was an outdoor theater. Six of the girls in the troupe and I put together an act which played at the Chase Hotel in St. Louis. We were just a line of girls who had been dancing at The Muny. Our costumes were just ordinary, nothing fancy, but it was my first experience doing an "act," and I enjoyed it enormously! The "show biz bug" had bitten me years ago, but it was biting harder as I got older, and believe me, it didn't hurt at all. I was liking it!

We girls would dance for the audience, and I still have one friend from that group. Her name is Katherine Burke. She went on to become a Rockette at the world famous Radio City Music Hall in New York City. We had an awful lot of fun doing our routines back then at my beloved Muny.

I remember one night about six weeks later, after we'd finished our routines, I'd gone upstairs and was walking down a long hallway to my dressing room when a man stepped out and began to speak to me.

"Are you in show business?" he asked, which I remember thinking was a sort of funny question, considering I was in full stage makeup and wearing a costume. I mean it's not as if women casually walked around like that. But I was raised to be polite and so answered "Yes, I am. I'm dancing in a show downstairs in the dinner room here."

"Well," he said, "I'm doing a club date here in the hotel tonight." ("Club dates" means it's a one-night act for a group of people.) "Well look," he went on. "Do you think you could come to watch my act tonight and see if maybe you could do it?"

"Sure," I said. He gave me all the details. I went to watch this man's act after I'd finished mine, and it really was very good. And for Vaudeville, the entertainment of that era, it was perfect.

The man's name was Andrew Mayo. His act was called "Pansy The Horse," and it consisted of two men dressed in a horse costume with a pretty girl whipping them, telling jokes and dancing a little.

I truly enjoyed watching his act that night and knew immediately I wanted to be a part of it, because it was really very funny. The audience loved it. They laughed and applauded and truly got a big kick out of that odd performance.

Getting laughs was very important to Vaudeville performers. If there were no laughs, it meant more long hours of rehearsals. Laughs were their bread and butter. It's what they lived for. It was all they performed for.

After the horse act was finished, I met with Mr. Mayo, who was the rear end of the horse, and said, "Yes, I can do this."

This young man said, "Well, that's fine. We open in Columbus, Ohio, in about six weeks. I'll keep in touch with you and will send you a contract and the bus fare to get you to Columbus." I knew I was making another step upward. Was I excited? Well, no. I don't excite easily, but I was happy with the way things were going.

I discussed this new career move with my parents who thought do the act with these men. But my mother wanted to go with me, and so she and I got on the bus and headed out to Columbus. Of course I had to be chaperoned, at least at the start of all of this. Columbus wasn't that far away, and we got there safely and into a hotel. I called the man who'd offered this job to me and found out I'd be performing in his act quite quickly, as soon as we'd rehearsed enough to get it down.

"Pansy The Horse" would be the second or third act of the evening. I recall being happy to discover that our first night out the main show's music would be played by an orchestra headed by Ozzie Nelson. His lead singer was Harriet Hilliard, and as the world now knows, they married and became very famous first on radio and then television with their "Ozzie and Harriet Show," along with their sons, Ricky and David. The Nelsons founded a dynasty of sorts because now their grandchildren are in show business---maybe even their great grandchildren at this point!

Rehearsals began and they were fine. Thanks to my early training in developing a strong sense of discipline, I learned my part and rehearsed without complaint. It went very well. My mother, finally satisfied that all was well and that I was safe, went back home to St. Louis.

We opened! I was worried about the act's being a hit, but as they always did, these worries, questions and fears vanished when I began to perform. Over the years, I've been asked frequently if the sound of applause was a "turn on," did it enhance my performance, give me a rush? Honestly, no.

On some level, a performer is always aware of the audience's reaction. But I just wanted to do my job and do it well, and even if there had been no applause, or even had there been only three people in the audience, I'd have still delivered a 100% performance for my audiences. I kept this credo all through my career too. I believed then as I do now those performers owe their audiences the very best show they can deliver. And that's what I did. Always.

Here's how that little Vaudeville show went: I'd walk out on the stage in my fetching costume, carrying a whip, and would turn to speak to the audience.

"Good evening, ladies and gentlemen," I'd begin, using the time-honored greeting. "I'd like to introduce you to a horse whose rare intelligence and beauty is acclaimed throughout the world. And here he is."

I'd then call out his name, "Pansy!!" while looking to stage left. Out would shuffle the two men in the horse suit.

"All right, Pansy," I'd say, "please show the audience how you can do this trick!" I'd name the trick and of course, Pansy would refuse to do it. I'd smack him on the feet or the rump with the whip and demand again that Pansy show the audience the trick. He wouldn't, so I'd hit him, and this time the man in the front end of the horse would jump up and wrap his legs around the back man and stand that way, perfectly still. The audience would howl with laughter.

Then, I'd pull a tub out on the stage and turn to Pansy and say "Now get up on that tub, do you hear me? Do it! Get UP ON THE TUB!!" Of course Pansy wouldn't do it and I'd swat him again and again. Pansy would never do the trick right, and would have to endure many blows from my whip. Don't forget now---this was Vaudeville. This kind of entertainment was really very good for its time.

The audiences loved us so much that we were able to get bookings in many other cities, like the Apollo Theater in Harlem where we appeared for one week. The great Ella FitzGerald was on the bill too. I remember that theater being awfully dirty, but even so, it was a good experience to have performed there.

I would travel with these two men in a big old black Packard with a suitcase containing the horse skin, several of my costumes (which they provided and I had to take very good care of,) and a bag with my personal stuff. I learned how to apply stage make-up during my Muny Opera days, and got very proficient at putting on false eyelashes.

We never changed that act. The name of the other man inside of Pansy besides Andrew Mayo, by the way, was Norni Morton. Eventually I took Andy's last name: Mayo. The reason was that his wife was in the show. I was going to replace her because she'd gotten pregnant and had to leave. (Bookers back then were adamant about acts not changing because they had to do promotions and advertising way ahead of time.) So if one of the act's principals had a name-change, it really got things messed up. There was always the danger that the bookings would be lost. Nor did those bookers want the act to evolve or change as it went along. They had to know in advance exactly what the act was about so they could sell and promote it, and the people hiring us would know precisely what they would be getting. So it seemed prudent for me to take Andy Mayo's last name, to replace his pregnant wife. I really didn't mind at all, and neither did my parents. It wasn't a Big Transition. I liked the name, and so just one day became

Virginia Mayo, and therefore wasn't Virginia Jones any longer. Well, I guess I'll always be Virginia Jones in my heart, but I never use that name anymore.

I was definitely on my own now, at the ripe old age of about 19. As time passed, I really became Virginia Mayo. I guess I'd left Virginia Jones back in St. Louis when I began traveling with these two men and my dog from hotel to hotel. After all, it doesn't matter what your name is as long as you have a sense of self and know who you are. I did then and I do now.

Anyway, it was a marvelous experience, and gave me a great head start on a show business career. All that traveling east of St. Louis let me see more of the United States than many other young people had ever had the opportunity to do. If I'd had I stayed in St. Louis, I'd never have seen it all.

My parents didn't object to my traveling alone with those men. They trusted me completely, and don't forget, the Great Depression was only just winding down. They were delighted I was bringing money into the family. I kept in close touch with my parents by mail, and because I knew where I'd be at each show, they could write to me there, in advance, sometimes sending letters to General Delivery. I'd begun sending home a portion of each of my paychecks. That was no problem for me. I'd never been extravagant and had need of nothing. My salary, a whopping $50. a week, was paid by the men who worked inside of Pansy, and all I had to pay for was my hotel room and my food. They took care of everything else. It was a completely platonic relationship and none of us ever thought of it as being anything else. I wasn't interested, and neither were they. We had a job to do. By the way, all of our names could not fit on most marquees. All that could fit beneath the name of the main act, was simply "Pansy the Horse." But on some marquees, all of our names would fit. The name of the act was the most important, though.

I was the "ring master" of the act. The two men always stayed inside of Pansy. I often wondered if they got hot in there, but it didn't matter because the act was always a big hit and we got many, many laughs.

We traveled around to different show places to put on our act. Ohio, Florida, Pennsylvania, Indiana, Maryland, New York, New Jersey, a whole lot of shows in Texas--everywhere. We performed in almost all of the big cities, and nearly always got in with the wonderful Big Bands so popular during those years. Benny Goodman. Glenn Miller. The Dorseys. Glen Gray and Artie Shaw. I got to hear them all and their music thrilled me just as good music today thrills me. I can't get enough of it.

One time we opened in New York City at the Warner Theater for a band headed by Leo Reisman who had a girl singer with whom I shared a dressing room. Her name was Dinah Shore and there was no way I could know that years later I'd find myself chatting with her on her very own TV talk Show, "The Dinah Shore Show." (Remember that? "See the USA – In your Chevrolet!" and that big, dramatic kiss she'd throw out to the TV audience?) Dinah was a classy lady and about the nicest of people, and we had great fun during that time. We also shared that same dressing room with a Chinese team called Toy and Wing. Dinah and Toy were on the bill, and it turned out that after their one performance, they were canceled. That left just Dinah and me.

It was during this time my beloved father died. His appendix had burst. Back then there was no penicillin or drugs that could heal him. They tried to operate, but it was just too late. He died. My dear, dear father. It was a horrible shock to me, and I immediately went home to be with my family. I couldn't believe it. My parents were my strongest support system and had always been there. Always. It was unthinkable that they'd actually ever die and leave me. But home I went to bury this man I loved so much, from whom I'd learned so much, and that was that. I went back to work.

The "Pansy the Horse" show stayed on for two weeks or more. Sometimes we'd stay in a town for weeks at a time, often performing in two towns in one week. I remember once opening for the famous Andrews Sisters. Patty is still my good friend today and we talk together frequently. Show business does give one great old friends with great old memories!

I never seemed to get tired of doing the Pansy act. Even though we had to keep things pretty much the same in each performance, (called a "standard" act,) it was always fresh and new for me. We continued to get laughs and that resulted in our getting more work. We got a lot of new jobs. When we could hear the laughter, we knew it would mean more work, but the laughs were the thing. They meant we were entertaining people, that they were loving us, and that combination always resulted in more work! It was a great "circle" and one I loved moving round and round in.

I well remember the Roxy Theater in New York City. I'll never be able to forget that wonderful place, (now torn down,) but not because we got to play it. I'd just gotten my darling new Boston Terrier whom I'd named "Dinky." I've always loved dogs, always have had dogs, and she was my darling. But I was having a little trouble housebreaking Dinky. After all, I walked her as much as I could, but I was in show business and because of that, my poor sweet puppy had to be left alone a lot. I know it was selfish for me to even get her, but dogs have always been a big part of my life, and I was and am always lonely without one or two around me.

Well, I thought I'd gotten the housebreaking situation pretty much under control because Dinky was finally behaving and doing her job outside. I'd finally been able to stop cleaning up after her. Good! My dear Dinkie was finally housebroken. I was so proud of her! My little Dinkie had finally learned to be a lady!

Or so I thought. I'll never forget one night at the Roxy when another performer knocked on my dressing room door, came in and in a fury, his face florid, steam all but coming out of his ears, announced "Your dog is doing her business in MY dressing room!" I was mortified! I'd thought she was trained, but she was sneaking off to the other guy's room and taking care of her bodily needs. Not good.

CHAPTER 4

Much to our enjoyment, the Pansy the Horse act got booked to do a show at the famous Radio City Music Hall in New York City. It was for the Christmas show. We were told it should fit in with the Spanish theme of the show. We worked there for seven weeks and had many early shows to do, also.

The reason they wanted our act to have a Spanish look about it was because the Radio City Music Hall stage show that year had a Spanish flavor, although the movie playing with it was "The Philadelphia Story" starring Katharine Hepburn, Cary Grant and Jimmy Stewart. (That great film definitely did not have a Spanish anything!) But the dancers, the Rockettes, were doing Spanish dancing, so we made Pansy the horse into a bull for that. I got a darling new costume out of the deal, too.

After the Radio City Music Hall show, we did our act with "Ol' Banjo Eyes," the famous singer, comedian and actor, Eddie Cantor. It was 1941. This time, at his request, we had to change Pansy's very sweet face with the big eyes and eyelashes so it would look like Eddie Cantor's face. Bigger eyes, as his were, (I'll never know how he rolled them around like that!) and of course, blackface. Now blackface would never do today because it would be considered stereotyping black people and making a mockery of them. Today, it would not be politically correct, but back then I regret to say that no one thought much about things like that. Well, no white people thought much of it that is, although I suspect it insulted a great many African Americans. Blackface meant that a white performer would cover his face and hands with heavy black make-up, sometimes the blackness applied with burnt corks. They would widely outline the lips in an exaggerated, wide, bright white shape spoofing the large lips of black people. I know it did ridicule black people, and I say with some embarrassment that it never occurred to me that African Americans back then would have felt demeaned by that's happening. It never occurred to me at all. But then, it didn't occur to anyone and while that doesn't make it right, it should be noted that those were very different times.

But amazingly, when Cantor did the act, he just didn't get laughs. Very unusual for him. He couldn't get them at all, and the act was a complete flop. Cantor was stymied. This was rare for the man who was used to having them "rollin' in the aisles." He was famous for making audiences howl with laughter and to applaud the house down. He was The Star of that era, and thought he'd be a big hit that time, but he just simply was not. It happens. Not all great performers can put on great shows all the time. Cantor really bombed.

And so it was I who was asked to step in. Me! To replace the great Eddie Cantor, and do our very same act. Eddie just continued to go on doing his usual performance, but dropped the horse bit. I have to say with all modestly that I was pretty good at doing that act, with the men now wearing a bull skin costume! Seven weeks was a very long time in that business.

I remember so vividly Eddie forcing all of us "lesser" actors and performers to stand behind him on that old stage, smiling and grinning like idiots while he did his entire act, singing "If You Knew Suzy Like I Knew Suzy, Oh! Oh! Oh What a Gal!" and all the other songs he made famous, prancing about, rolling his huge, bulging eyeballs. It was exhausting for us to have to stand there, posing, grinning, looking interested, for much more than an hour. We were already exhausted from doing our own performances after all, but he was Eddie Cantor and that's what he wanted, so that's what he got. It was awful. But thank God he finally decided he didn't want to do that show any longer, and he quit it, so we were free. What a relief!

But something very interesting was going on in that show. In the cast of "Banjo Eyes" was a young lady who had a very small part. She was dark-haired and beautiful, someone you'd definitely notice. (She kind of stood with her feet like a duck, as I recall.) I clearly remember she kept staring at me all the time during the show. I remember feeling slightly uncomfortable about her doing that, but I ignored her and went on with the show. Eventually I found out why she kept watching me. It was years later that she wrote a smashing best seller and she often said publicly that she'd based her central character half on Judy Garland and half on me. The dark-haired, beautiful young lady staring at me all the time never made it in show business, but she did make it big as an author. She was named Jacqueline Susanne and she wrote "Valley of the Dolls."

But Vaudeville wasn't all glamour! Actually it was a very hard part of my career. I had to take the subway from 25th Street to the Music Hall, which is located on Sixth Avenue, and I was always late getting into my dressing room, something I hated. Being on time and prepared was and still is of primary importance to me. I am just rigid on this subject. You show up on time, know your lines, do the work. Anyway, I'd rush to get my make-up and costume on and would run onto the stage.

After the Cantor show at Radio City Music Hall, "my boys" and I got booked into Billy Rose's Diamond Horseshoe, a new show in New York City. We'd definitely arrived!

CHAPTER 5

Billy was really a wonderful man, an incredible showman and he truly knew how to put on a great show! Not everyone in life gets to know a character like that, but I got lucky—I did. He was amazing!

Billy Rose was putting on an extremely funny show called "Mrs. Astor's Pet Horse," so the "Pansy men" or "the boys" as I lovingly called them, decided to try to get him to see our act, or at least to tell him about it. They thought it would be a good fit with Billy's "Mrs. Astor's" show. Our agent got an appointment and Billy said he'd see them and he listened to what the boys had to say about our act. He told them "Well, I guess maybe I can use you guys after I see the act, but you'll have to lose the girl." Oh no! Billy Rose didn't want me. I was crushed when I heard that. I'd worked hard and I knew the audiences loved my performance.

But those boys, my boys, were wonderful and told him no, absolutely not. They could not and would not break up the act. It wouldn't be right and besides, my part in "Pansy the Horse" was completely vital to the act. In fact, they said, there was no act without my part. Sorry, they said, but we can't do that. (Imagine! These two young nobodies stood up to the famous Billy Rose. And for me!) I guess Billy hadn't really had people do that to him very often, so he listened.

"But Mr. Rose," they suggested to Billy, "why don't you meet her? When you do, you'll understand why there is just no possibility of our not having her in the act." And so that's how in 1941, I got to meet the world-famous Billy Rose.

I won't forget what Billy Rose said when he met me and saw the act. "Oh, my mistake!" he said. "I can sure use her!" Billy Rose was impressed with me. Me! I was beyond flattered. This guy was world famous and everyone in that business wanted to be in his shows!

Billy Rose gave me a part, but alas, not with "my boys." I felt pretty awful about that, because they'd given me my start, and I'd loved traveling with them and doing "Pansy the Horse." I won't ever forget that they'd defended my being in their act insisting its not being doable unless I was in it. I'm forever grateful to them, but unfortunately, the act had run its course and was now defunct.

I was on my way. My first really big break! As it turned out, a great deal of this new show I'd be in really rested on my shoulders. It was a revue, showcasing dancers and singers and other performers, and was called "Billy Rose's Diamond Horseshoes," at his famous Diamond Horseshoe nightclub. The show was staged by a very famous man, famous for his directorship and staging. His name was John Murray Anderson. I was, well nearly, the star of it! It was amazing. Great notices. Lots of audiences! And people were coming backstage all the time to meet me and praise the show. I was just incredibly happy.

Suddenly I was getting a lot of publicity. I was given a big spread in Look Magazine which is no longer in business, but it was a very famous magazine back then. I was wearing fabulous costumes and dancing on fabulous stages and meeting fabulous people! I was not especially star-struck, mind you. I knew I had a big job to do. But I can't deny I was pretty delighted over how it was all happening.

Without my knowing it at first, (and I only found out because the other performers had heard about it and told me,) Billy Rose one day called Sam Goldwyn and invited him to come and see the show.

"You've got to come see this girl," he is reported to have told Goldwyn. Sam Goldwyn was in New York looking for new talent.

Goldwyn had helped in the founding of MGM and made a number of hit films, amongst them "Wuthering Heights" with Merle Oberon and (later Sir and even later Lord) Laurence Olivier. He also made the endlessly wonderful "The Best Years of our Lives," both classics that will live forever and are played over and over on TV today. I got to be in the second one, "The Best Years of Our Lives" and it hasn't hurt me a bit. I'm honored to have had a part in that movie. My experience in that excellent film is why I named this book "The Best Years of My Life."

I thought it was wonderful that Billy Rose had asked Sam to come to see me perform, which he did, and asked me to come to his office to speak with him the next day. I said I'd go to see him, but I that day, I didn't get a chance to shower or get cleaned up from the show when I went to keep my appointment with the great man, and I remember my hair being awfully dirty. So I put on a hat to cover it. Of course it was the first thing Goldwyn asked of me — to please remove my hat so he could see my face.

"But I don't want to," I groused. "My hair is so dirty and I don't want you to see it like that." But he prevailed. (I've always been very fussy about

24

my hair and want it to look beautiful and perfect all the time.) But, people didn't usually disregard what Sam Goldwyn wanted them to do, so I reluctantly, I removed my hat.

The man looked me all over and then said The Words!, The Words all actors dream of hearing; "I'd like to make a screen-test of you." As I said, people usually didn't say no to Sam Goldwyn. I surely didn't! And of course now I'm pretty glad I took that hat off.

So many star-struck young girls came out to Hollywood back then, (today too, I know,) and spent a lot of time sitting on benches, never getting discovered. I've often wondered about the vast amount of talent this country has offered to entertainment industries like the movies, that hasn't been tapped. But there I was in my very early twenties, being offered a screen test by one of the most powerful moguls in Hollywood and America. You can imagine what my answer was! You'd be right!

Then, the icing on the cake. Only it was like globs of icing piled thick on an enormous cake. Someone told me that David O. Selznick was in New York City looking for talent too, and also wanted to see me. (I'm not sure if he'd seen the show as Sam Goldwyn had. Perhaps Selznick had just been told it was good.) Thus I went to see him in his office also. Imagine that! Billy Rose, then Sam Goldwyn and then David O. Selznick. Talk about your cup runnething over!

Mr. Selznick asked me if I thought I'd be any good in the movies. "Well," I answered, "I'd like to try the movies. Sure."

"What's your name?" he asked me, and in my confusion I said "Virginia Jones." "But we've already got a Jones. You can't be Jones," he said somewhat gruffly as if I'd deliberately done something wrong. Of course I couldn't possibly know he was speaking of the luminous, beautiful Jennifer Jones who would one day be his wife. (She was about to make that remarkable movie, "Song of Bernadette.") I recovered my cool and told him I was really Virginia Mayo now. He seemed pleased at the name, nodded and accepted it without comment.

When Selznick said, "It's my intention to make a screen-test of you," I remember feeling a little weak in the knees.

I did one. He brought in a Hollywood photographer who took an awful lot of film of me and made me look wonderful. I'll just never forget that, how incredibly great he made me look. I was simply stunned! That was me looking back from the mirror? Little Virginia Clara Jones from St. Louis, Missouri? Well, I guess it was. I was moving forward and I was loving it!

Like a tennis ball, I went back and forth between the two famous movie men, Goldwyn and Selznick. I then did an acting test for Goldwyn, but I wasn't too good and I knew it. I really hadn't had too much experience, after all. No coaching save for dear old Aunt Alice. But the two men got together and I heard later that Mr. Selznick said to Mr. Goldwyn, "I don't think I'm going to take Miss Mayo's option up now. I think she has great possibilities for the screen, but she needs some acting experience." He let Goldwyn have me, figuring Goldwyn could do more for me. The two men were friends.

The decision was made. I'd go with Goldwyn. I knew I very much needed acting lessons, and he'd provide them for me. As I look back now, I am very aware that I was just another in a long line of so-called "beauties" that Sam intended to mold and hammer and beat into perhaps being his very first leading lady. I was willing to take what he offered.

I was given a "charm coach" of all things, a woman named Eleanor King who would work on my overall appearance, my posture and attitude. They told me I had a "natural beauty" but that my face was too full for the camera and so they'd have to sculpture it, make it more "contoured." Thank heaven they didn't send me off for surgery! No, instead my face got a daily massage. Sam Goldwyn gave me acting lessons, speech, voice, and dance lessons. I had to go on a diet! And during this huge regimen, Sam called me every night to see if I was definitely keeping up with all my lessons, and of all things to be sure I'd brushed my hair one hundred strokes! I'll tell you, back then, you earned your place in the sun!

Well, apparently I improved enough in about six months of all this so I could finally be tested again. But I seemed to freeze a little when the camera turned my way. This is not good for the movie business! But in time I warmed up and lost my stage (or camera) fright.

CHAPTER 6

Our country was at war. Pearl Harbor had been bombed by the Japanese on December 7th, 1941. The whole country was mobilized working for "the cause," and there I was, booked on a train going to California. I had been given an upper berth, which I thought was pretty cheesy of Mr. Goldwyn. He could have sprung for a plane ticket. That man would try to save a buck now and again, even though he was a multimillionaire!

I had Dinky with me too, but she had to stay in a boxcar down the line which upset me greatly because I worried about her a lot. She was scared, I know, but I did go back there to visit her often and I think that soothed her somewhat. I wish they didn't do that to dogs, but I guess other passengers had to be considered.

I arrived in Hollywood in January or February and the studio people from Goldwyn were right there to meet me, thank heaven, because looking around, standing there with my little dog and my luggage, I felt as if I had landed on another planet. Sun was there; lots of hot sun, and palm trees and endless lines of expensive cars. I hadn't ever seen anything like this! I tried to act sophisticated and worldly but I'm not so sure I was carrying it off too well.

The Goldwyn gentlemen walked me to a car and drove me to where I would be staying. To my delight I discovered I'd be living in the very famous Mae West's Raven's Wood apartment building in Hollywood. I was really impressed! I'd had no idea at all that they'd put me up in her apartment. I mean she was hugely famous. Imagine! Me, living in Mae West's apartment! I could hardly believe what was happening to me. I got all my luggage in there and Dinky too and I want to tell you, I felt just wonderful. Like a queen!

The next day, the bubble abruptly burst. The people who'd brought me there returned. They rang the doorbell and when I answered, they told me I had to leave. Leave! Where would I go? I stood there stunned. I didn't know anything at all about Hollywood. And furthermore, I wanted to know why! How come I was getting kicked out when I'd just gotten there? What was going on here? After floating around on clouds, I was quite suddenly crashing to earth and I had no idea why.

I soon found out. It was because of Dinky. Mae West owned the apartment building and she had a strong and unshakable rule—--No Dogs Allowed. Ever.

Well, I've explained about my love of dogs. All dogs. Especially my dogs. There was no way I was going to give up my dog. Not for Mae West, and not for her apartment. No. I'd rather be kicked out into the street than to even consider getting rid of my beloved dog Dinky. No way! No.

But they found a place for me, those people did, and it was one that accepted dogs, thank God. It was a fine apartment and I was happy there as long as I had dear Dinky. It was a close call, but I can truly tell you I would have walked the streets rather than abandon or give away my beloved Dinky.

But another problem surfaced. I realized quite quickly I'd need a car in Hollywood. I walked around a lot while I was waiting to hear from the studio, and knew I simply had to have a car. There was not then, nor is there now, a network of public transportation in California and certainly not in Hollywood. I could walk to a nearby drugstore and could eat my dinner there at least, but I was beginning to feel forsaken, desolate. I didn't know what to do. I knew I would have to get a car, but how? I'd never owned a car before but at least I'd learned how to drive and had gotten my license.

I got in touch with my dear mother. She'd know what to do. She was alone now because of my beloved father's death, so I asked her to come out to be with me. It really seemed like a good idea, to have her here. I was so lonely and scared out in California and was feeling ignored by Sam Goldwyn who'd been the one to bring me out there in the first place.

Mother came out and began to live with me. We found another apartment in The Hollywood Towers, again a place that would take dogs, and she happily cooked for me and cared for Dink. And eventually, I got myself a car! Life was beginning to look a little better.

I remember being asked by the studio people if I'd be willing to attend a Canteen and to dance with soldiers and sailors. These affairs were what the USO's would put together for young men about to leave to fight in World War II. Maybe even to die. And a lot did. Of course I agreed to go.

Naturally the men at the Canteens wanted to dance with the already very famous stars like Rita Hayworth, Lana Turner, Betty Grable, June Allyson, Carole Landis, Ginger Rogers, Hedy Lamarr, Dorothy Lamour, Esther Williams, Jane Powell, Ann Miller and the like, but even though I'd just arrived and thus far was a "nobody," I got a number of partners too. I did what I could to cheer up these young men who obviously had it very much on their minds that they might well be on their way to die for their country. Those dances were great fun, and I well remember them. I remember those kids, too. Oh, they were so young. So was I, in fact, and so it didn't seem so odd as it was happening, but as I look back, I realize they were just babies, those dear guys, and they fought in a huge war and many of them never came home. Or if they did, they came home with parts of themselves missing, often parts of their minds. We do not fully appreciate the horrors of war, unless we've lived through one.

But before the momentous event of my getting a car of my own back in 1942, I found a friend who'd drive me back and forth to work in her car. Every day. Imagine! I was mobile, thanks to her, and I'll never forget her kindness to me. Her name was Amelita Ward. I could get to the studio (they finally set up acting lessons for me, and even charm lessons. Learning to walk into a room and sit down properly and all those things a "lady" has to know, especially a lady on the silver screen!) There were a number of people working on me and I was learning. It was a tough haul, but I learned quickly and I always did believe in hard study and hard work and getting the job done. And, I had signed a five-year contract with Sam Goldwyn in New York.

My life was again about to change drastically. One day when I didn't have much to do, I ambled over to look at the stage where a very interesting picture was being filmed. It was a movie called "Jack London," and was the life story of that famous author. I suddenly found myself asking the director for a small part. I knew a part was available, and made up my mind I wanted it. It was of a young girl, perfect for me, and so I went straight up to the director and told him I wanted it! Amazingly, he looked me over and simply said, "OK. Go to wardrobe and get tested for your costumes." And that was that! I got my first part just by asking. You see? In life you quite often have to grab for what you want. This still very famous movie was being filmed at the Goldwyn studios and also starred that wonderful actress, the then young and so lovely Susan Hayward.

This movie was a biography of the author, and my part was very small. I played the part of Jack London's very first love. I wanted him, but eventually for many reasons, it turned out he didn't want me, (in the film, that is) and so he walked out of my life with my standing under an umbrella yelling that he was "yella" or something! Oh, when I see that old black and white film and see how incredibly young I was, I'm just boggled. It's just amazing, watching yourself mature on film.

Anyway, the star of this movie, the man who played Jack London was a man named Michael O'Shea. I first saw him sitting on a curb on the set, his elbow on his knee, head resting on his hand. He looked so darling, I thought, so sweet and kind. And it turned out that he in fact was a sweet and kind man, and very handsome. He had a look in his eye I found completely irresistible. Later, he would become my beloved husband, and the father of our only child, our adorable and dearly loved Mary.

CHAPTER 7

I got myself another part in a movie. Things were beginning to look pretty good. It was with RKO, so I'd be loaned to them by Sam Goldwyn, a common practice amongst studios then and now, and I didn't even have to audition! They just took me at face value. This was a good omen.

It was a cute little picture, called "Seven Days Ashore." There were no "stars" in this movie, just contract people such as I was, and it was filmed at RKO. I vividly recall one scene where we had to fall into the water at night and we nearly froze.

Sam Goldwyn told me to hurry on back after "Seven Days Ashore," telling me he intended to give me lots more acting lessons, that he liked the work I'd done in "Seven Days Ashore," and had big plans for me. He tested me for "The Princess and the Pirate" which would also star the already world famous Bob Hope. In it, I was a King's daughter running away from him to marry the man I love. Obviously it was a comedy. Oh, those crazy plots! Well, it was up to all of us in the business to make everything believable to our public. And OK, the plots weren't rocket science, but they were entertaining movies and people loved them, and I surely loved making them!

Mr. Goldwyn told me that because of my very good work in "Seven Days Ashore," I was ready and could do "The Princess and the Pirate." I knew Mr. Goldwyn was right, I really was ready to do "The Princess and the Pirate." But I had to test for that picture because another actress was being considered. I won! Bob Hope, of course, was an awful lot of fun to work with. He had an endless supply of jokes he fed to me which I'd dutifully repeat, even though they weren't always in the script. (Sometimes he'd improvise "pages" of script that weren't there. The man was, and remains, a genius.) He always had a cadre of writers nearby who'd feed him ideas, and he'd be off and running. This man was unstoppable, and today, in his mid-nineties, he still is! Honestly I think this movie was one of his best because he had an endless amount of very funny visual things he could do. He kept us laughing a lot on that set.

Sam Goldwyn gave me a five-year contract. There was very little money offered, but "little money" was only offered to every new actor or actress back then, when they were just starting out. I got $100. a week from the Goldwyn studios, but that was OK, it was fine. I knew I had to pay my dues in this industry and work hard if I wanted fame and fortune. The money would come later, I hoped, and my mother and I could live pretty well on that $100.00 a week. Don't forget, it was the early 1940's.

Mr. Sam Goldwyn had a very annoying habit, and I've thought and thought about it over the years and really haven't been able to truly get it straight in my head or figure out why he did this: He began calling me into his office often. Often? Continually would be a better word. I'd get the word he wanted to see me, and my heart would sink. Off I'd trudge for another session on the carpet. He would complain endlessly about my work. No matter how well I did, no matter how good the reviews, he'd complain about it. He'd tell me he didn't like my work, my acting, my posture, my everything. He'd say "Your voice was bad in that scene," or, "You didn't move well in that movie," or, "You looked too nervous" in some of those scenes in "The Princess and the Pirate." Nervous? What did he expect? I had to look nervous—after all, pirates were attacking us, for heaven's sake! What was I supposed to do, stand there grinning at them? That man drove me nuts.

Goldwyn would have me look at the rushes, (the term "rushes" means yesterday's film, and it was when people working on the movie check out the day's work,) and he would point out where, in his overblown opinion, I'd gone wrong. Very occasionally, (make that rarely,) he'd tell me I'd done a good job in a certain scene. Really, I'll never truly understand why he kept picking on me that way. He should have done it to an actor like maybe Danny Kaye who had real attitude problems and needed to be brought down. A lot! But not I. I was new and trying my best and I had no attitude! All I wanted out of this was to work and do my work well. Goldwyn would even call me at my apartment and demand I show up in his office at a certain time, usually within a few minutes, and once again, off I'd go. He was very intimidating to me. For five years I had Sam Goldwyn hanging around my neck like that dead albatross in "The Rhyme of the Ancient Mariner." Maybe he had some dumb idea all of this harassment would toughen me up. Maybe it would make me want to work harder and succeed even more, make me as driven and crazy as all those other famous lady moviestars. Well, I did succeed and it was in no way because of Sam Goldwyn's abuse.

After he'd finish his tirade, I'd walk out and look down the hall and see a long line of other employees quaking, awaiting their turns to get yelled

32

at. I have no idea why Goldwyn did this, but as I said, I've thought a lot about it over the years and have concluded that it maybe was his way to keep actors in line, to make sure they regarded him as their father and king and benevolent (and sometimes not so benevolent) dictator. Maybe he had a serious need to display his power over the actors and actresses in his employ. Everyone was afraid of him, not only me. I'll tell you though, he never once made me cry and I never ever told him I was sorry and that I'd do better. I stood my ground, took the crap he dished out and went back to work. I suppose this behavior of his was, as the kids say today, "a power thing."

And speaking of Danny Kaye, I was asked to test to appear in his movie "Up In Arms," but I didn't pass the test, and so they gave that part to Connie Dowling. I got stuck, demoted down in that movie to being a "Goldwyn Girl," a chorus of girls, all really beautiful young ladies, but not thought of as being particularly bright. I hated being thought of like that. Many wannabe actresses did get to be Goldwyn Girls but unfortunately never went much beyond that. It made me feel demeaned to have to do that.

Dinah Shore was also in "Up In Arms," and it would have been great fun to be with her again, but it was not to be and really, without any sour grapes I can truthfully say I'm glad I didn't get that part. I did work with Kaye in a lot of other films later on, however. ("Wonder Man" in 1945, "The Kid from Brooklyn" in 1946, "The Secret Life of Walter Mitty" in 1947 and "A Song is Born" in 1948. I was working simultaneously on "The Best Years of Our Lives" while doing the Mitty movie. That was hard work!)

Everybody loved Danny Kaye, but believe me, he wasn't all that easy to be around. He was demanding. But, he was Goldwyn's pet. No, he was Goldwyn's cash cow!

I guess to keep me in line, and the other people he loved (so he thought, and so he said,) Sam Goldwyn could sometimes be extremely kind to me, too. It was his way of keeping me and his other acting employees totally off balance. Stern lecture, kind gesture. Bawling out, sympathetic father. It was an endless dance with that guy.

I'll never forget how Sam Goldwyn (he was obviously in one of his "kindly father" moods) once sent Connie Dowling and me to Adrian's Salon. Now Adrian was an extremely famous Hollywood "dresser." You can still see his name in the credits of many of the old movies. Anyway, Sam sent us to Adrian's shop to pick out clothes for our personal wardrobe. We were stunned. (I think both of us had recently had a sound drubbing from SG.) Off we went and bought our new clothes and we wore them often. It was wonderful of Mr. Goldwyn to do that for us, and showed that he really did have a good heart. I think!

Anyway, when he was in his "kindly" mode, he would frequently invite me to his home for dinner parties, and his wife, Frances, a dear, kind, wonderful woman would personally drive to my apartment, pick me up, take me to the party and bring me home. (This was before I got my own car.) She was always doing things like that. I loved her a lot, and I won't ever forget her.

The parties were fun and dizzying to me, a young girl out of St. Louis. At least during those parties Sam didn't scold me. He treated me with respect and kindness at those affairs. It was very, very odd.

I remember one night at his long dining room table, they sat me next to George Cukor. Me! Imagine! I didn't know what to say to him. What could I possibly say to one of the most famous directors in the world? I opted to say nothing.

The Goldwyns lived in a huge mansion, of course, in Beverly Hills, pretty opulent but not nearly as opulent as Jack Warner's, I was to discover later on. The Goldwyns, by all Hollywood standards, were pretty conservative. They'd come from very poor backgrounds and had lived through the Depression, so they were careful with money even if they did have servants and a swimming pool and everything else in the American Dream. (If you get a chance, do read "Goldwyn" by A. Scott Berg, because it tells of Sam Goldwyn's remarkable journey into show business. I don't think there's another story like it.)

To show how the Goldwyns weren't interested in the flashy wealthy Hollywood lifestyle, Mrs. Goldwyn drove around in a not very new Dodge, for example. She was very cultured and proper and always associated herself with the nicer elements of Hollywood, and I know if I'd been wild and woolly and had misbehaved and had raised hell and made a bad name for myself, she would not have had me to her parties. I was always a lady. My mother made sure of that. I've always tried to be a lady at all times.

And now as I think back about some of the parties, I remember another one—a dinner party at Jack Warner's. I'd recently returned from England after filming Captain Horatio Hornblower with the wonderful, classy, beautiful Gregory Peck. I'd just turned thirty and Jack decided to have a birthday party for me, and oh, it was just so elegant. He was far more elegant than Goldwyn was. Anyway, I sat on Jack's left, and on my right was Clark Gable! Now, Clark was a very nice man, but had no desire to pay any attention to me at all, because he was so preoccupied with his new wife who was seated across from him, Lady something or other. I forget her name now. It was a wonderful evening and so nice of the Warners to do that for me. I liked Jack Warner but never had the relationship with him I had with Goldwyn. Sam Goldwyn was really my mentor and when he wasn't calling me on the carpet for this and that, he was good to me. After all, he gave me all those great parts!

CHAPTER 8

Along around this time, I had an unusual experience. Well, I guess not "unusual" because it goes on all the time now, and did then, too. It was upsetting, however. My mother and I attended a nearby First Presbyterian Church. (This was obviously before I became a Catholic.) Many other actresses and actors attended that church too, and the minister at the time was Pastor Louis Evans. He asked me once if I'd appear in a play to be performed at the church which he'd written called, I think, "The Woman at the Well." I willingly agreed, since rehearsals and the play itself wouldn't interfere with my regular acting jobs. This play would star my old friend Rhonda Fleming, another buddy, Dennis Morgan, a famous character actor named Porter Hall, and my husband Michael O'Shea would be in it too. (Rhonda had been raised by a Mormon family, but First Presbyterian was the church she chose to attend.)

We did the play right up in front of the altar in front of the congregation. So there we all were, looking very religious and spiritual, wearing Biblical costumes, and telling this wonderful story our minister had written.

I'll never forget what happened when we went back to our dressing rooms after the play ended; we'd been robbed! Right there in the church! Watches, jewelry, money. All gone. Imagine, right there in that sacred place! I still can't get over it. We never got anything back, but it kind of does make you wonder, right? I mean to be robbed in church of all places! What is, what was, our world coming to? Well, I certainly have had a lot of laughs along the way and this was one too, even thought it was awful when it happened.

I was getting through the second year of my contract with Goldwyn studios and was scheduled to star in "Wonder Man" in 1945 with Danny Kaye. Danny sort of remembered me from being one of the Goldwyn Girls in his "Up In Arms" movie, so I was glad to have a starring role now because believe me, I hated being a Goldwyn Girl! It had a terrible connotation because all you had to do or be to qualify was to be beautiful. (And classy, according to Goldwyn.) In other words, beautiful and dumb. Ugh. I had a lot more to offer the world than that, I can tell you! I certainly did.

I'd met Danny Kaye during my Vaudeville days at the Baltimore Theater in Maryland. Danny was the headliner and we were called in to add more comedy because frankly, he wasn't doing so well. Let's be honest; he was bombing. So in we went with our act, and we wowed 'em as we always did, Pansy, the boys and I! I remember Danny's coming to my dressing room to thank us back then, and to say goodbye, and then he turned to me and said it was so nice working with me. I liked him all right back then.

I remember one evening after a performance at Billy Rose's Diamond Horseshoe, I went to watch Danny perform just before I was about to leave for California and my new movie career. I recall having to find a girl who'd fill in for me. The money from Billy Rose wasn't all that good and so it wasn't easy to find someone, but I did, and so I knew I could, with a clear conscience, head out to California. It was a nice girl, a Canadian named Frances Diamond, married, and she was thrilled to get that part. Unfortunately, Billy Rose didn't take a shine to her as he had to me, and she never went anywhere with it. I was the lucky one! Oh, and maybe I had some talent too. Heck, Billy Rose and Sam Goldwyn immediately picked me out of a crowd, so I must have really had something.

Danny Kaye did remember me when we began to work on "Wonder Man" together, and obviously he wasn't happy to be reminded (by seeing me) that he'd flopped in Baltimore. Hey! It happens.

Sylvia Kaye wrote all the songs her husband Danny performed and it was clear they'd rehearse at home because he had those magically, maniacally delivered songs down pat. And those incredible dialogues! He was the master of all that. The best. No one could touch him then or now. Today Robin Williams has that kind of frenetic energy too, although in my opinion, he can't do the imitation foreign languages that Kaye could do. Sid Caesar came pretty close.

But even though Danny and I had an excellent chemistry on screen, he really didn't like me much and was always asking for another actress. Even when we worked on "The Secret Life of Walter Mitty," and "A Song is Born," he wanted someone else. (I wonder what he thought about his wanting to replace me when those two movies became smash hits.)

For example, Danny wanted Ingrid Bergman for the Mitty movie. Of the two, she might have been kind of a fit with the Mitty film, but let's face it. Bergman was a wonderful and extremely talented actress, but in a comedy like that? Or comedy at all? I don't think so. Her being in that role is unimaginable! She was a serious, somewhat dour Scandinavian. Hardly ever smiled. I don't know what Danny was thinking. Remember Bergman in "Cactus Flower?" She was terrible and didn't help that picture at all.

But in any case, regardless of Kaye's protestations, I stayed on those films with him and they did very, very well. They're still being played constantly on television. So much for Danny Kaye and his not liking me to be in his movies. Ha!

I hope I never seem ungrateful for the opportunity I had to play in those marvelous movies. The work was hard, yes, and the lights so bright they'd burn my eyes, so hot they'd burn my skin, even from as far away as they were. But it was fun, a kind of fun no other people really get to have except people who work in this medium. I know I've been given a lot more magic in my life than many people have, and I am never ungrateful. I never took it, or take it, for granted. It's been a perfectly wonderful gift to me.

CHAPTER 9

I know you have noticed, as I have, that the population in our country seems to be inordinately obsessed with people's love lives, and most especially the love lives of the famous. In fact, it seems to me that people are more interested in the love lives of personalities on TV and in the movies than, I think, they are in their own. People just think too much about movie stars. I know it's hard to believe, but we're normal human beings just like everyone else and just because we appear on a movie screen does not make us any better, smarter, wiser or more knowledgeable than anyone else. It displeases me greatly when I read or hear that people today know everything about someone famous in the film or TV industry, but can't find Canada on a map, don't know the names of our most powerful leaders in Government, can't name a famous book, tell who Abraham Lincoln was, when World War II was, or what it was all about. It is appalling, our young people's lack of knowledge, and no one seems to care in the least. I have no idea why kids today are graduated from highschool or even college without the basic fundamentals of education. Many of them can't even put a decent (or correct) sentence together properly. It's a huge disgrace and in this regard, I am embarrassed for America.

However, having said that, I'll say here that I know my fans were interested in my love life and would like this to be a tell-all book. Well, believe it or not, folks, there isn't a heck of a lot to tell. Sorry! I met Mike O'Shea when we worked together on "Jack London." I fell in love with him, and after many years we married, had Mary and he died. That's about it. Pretty cut and dried.

I was twenty-six when we married, and really hadn't dated much. Frankly I just didn't much like most men. They had to be perfect for me to have an interest. I remember Gary Cooper used to follow me around in his big, expensive car in those enormous outdoor studio areas Goldwyn had built, and I would turn and glare at him and wonder "what on earth is he doing that for?" He'd smile that crooked smile he'd honed to such perfection, raise his eyebrows, lower his head and do his famous and appealing (or so he thought) Gary Cooper "aw shucks" routine, but I wasn't impressed or especially moved to speak to him. I'd just keep on walking and he'd keep on driving, just behind me. I can still hear the low rumble of his big automobile's engine as he openly stalked me from that magnificent convertible car of his. Today, that car is taken around to museums and car shows all over the country, along with poster-sized photos of him standing by it looking aw shucksie again. Well, it was a gorgeous car, but truly I didn't want to have anything to do with him, or it. He wasn't good to women. He loved 'em and left 'em. I remember vividly going to England with a group of people including Patricia Neal. She'd just appeared with Cooper in "The Fountainhead," that remarkable story by Ayn Rand. Pat had fallen madly, deeply, passionately in love with Gary, and from the way he behaved toward her, she was certain he felt the same way about her. Well, the movie came to an end and so did the affair. It was soon after that, that we had to go to England for a command performance, and Pat was in horrible shape—just terrible. She was torn to pieces by that man, her poor heart just destroyed, and I doubt she ever got over it. I will speak more about this later.

Males had to have something really very special going for them before I'd even consider liking them. Oh, I remember I had a boyfriend somewhere along the way, but I can't even remember his name. I was focused on my career mostly. I wanted to be a big success and there wasn't time for dating. Truly, there just wasn't. Work began very early in the morning and went on until late at night, and if anyone else was able to go out partying after that and still look fresh and in control the next day, my hat is off to them. Not I. I had other things to do, and one of them was to sleep a lot, and of course, to fall in love with Michael O'Shea. I did that. I fell in love with that handsome man almost immediately. He was forty-one, fifteen years my senior. He'd been married before and had already had children. But on July 7, 1947, he and I became man and wife. But I will talk more about this part of my life later on.

CHAPTER 10

After "Seven Days Ashore," I made another movie for Sam Goldwyn. It was then 1945 and this movie was called "Wonder Man" and I made it after "The Princess and the Pirate."

It was after "Wonder Man," that I met a man who would become a dear friend for all the rest of my life, and his life too, right up until he died. His name was Steve Cochran and I loved him. (Like a brother.) He was tall, and in spite of the fact that he photographed as if he was a really big man, he wasn't. Steve was a man with a slight frame, had unusually dark, deeply smoldering eyes, thick black eyebrows, black hair, and was often cast as a gangster or a rough, hard man. Steve was none of those things in real life. He was polite and sensitive, and very kind. But indeed, he was extremely sexy and women just couldn't get enough of him. I loved acting with him, and we went on to make many films together, including the famous "White Heat" with James Cagney in 1949.

I know there's been speculation over the years that I had an affair with Steve Cochran, but I didn't. Perhaps the thought crossed my mind from time to time, but he was married, and besides, he had so many girlfriends behind his wife's back, I'm not so sure I could have really fit in with his very busy schedule!

But anyway, we made our movies together and we were such good friends. We even appeared together later on in Warner Brothers movies. I miss him so much.

Steve loved to go out to sea. He had a boat and at the time of his death, he was no longer under contract. He took some women with him on a boat ride one afternoon, allegedly to photograph them for a possible screen test. He had a heart attack while at sea and those poor women had no idea how to drive (or sail) that boat back to shore. They must have panicked terribly. Eventually, they did get help but poor Steve was gone. It was too late to save him. It's a very sad story. I miss him so much. I think had he lived longer, he and I would have remained friends to the end of our lives. In my mind, I can just see him in my home now, with us talking and talking about the good old days. He was a darling man.

It seemed like my movies were all but back to back and in fact they were. "Wonder Man" also starred my dear friend Vera Ellen, that wondrous presence and dancer. Sheer energy! It was her first movie, and Steve Cochran's first with Goldwyn. It was also in color. I so loved working with my two good friends, Vera and Steve. They've left me with dear memories and I think about them every single day.

I then made "The Kid from Brooklyn," also in color, which starred Lionel Stander, dear Vera Ellen again, Eve Arden (she would go on to great fame as "Our Miss Brooks" on the radio which also starred Jeff Chandler who went on to much bigger things as a film actor) as the teacher she could never get to be interested in her.

I found I was getting more and more roles now, and they were frequently starring parts, to my delight. And then came that great classic, "The Best Years of our Lives." I am inordinately proud of that film and still feel a great sense of pride when I see it on TV. This film was about four military men returning from World War II. A haunting, memorable movie, it has never gone out of style, and while my part, Marie, was that of an insensitive, flighty air-headed wife to Dana Andrews' character, it was one of the best parts I ever had. Oh, the cast of that film was fabulous; Dana Andrews (who played my husband) Myrna Loy, Frederick March, Teresa Wright, Cathy O'Donnell, Hoagie Carmichael, and of course Harold Russell, the one who represented the navy in the film, and also the man who had in fact had his hands blown off during World War II. He played that exact role in the film. There is nothing I'd change about that movie. It is probably the most watched film in film history and never fails to move audiences to tears.

After the filming of "The Best years of Our Lives" was finished, I recall John Huston telling me I should have gotten an Oscar for my role playing Dana Andrews' wife. I wasn't a very good or decent wife in that role. Marie wasn't exactly a sympathetic character, but I played her well. I was supposed to convey that I'd had a great deal of freedom while Dana was off fighting the war, and I wasn't about to give all that up just because he'd returned. Marie was a young woman who'd become very used to "partying," as the kids say today, and was angry that her poor battle-weary husband just simply wanted to take off his uniform and get back into a normal, war-free life. She wanted him to leave the uniform on, so she could show him off. Marie wanted to kick up her heels. Her husband wanted to pretend the war had never happened, to settle down, get a job and raise a family. In time, he fell in love with Teresa Wright's character.

It was an honor to have appeared in that film and it won an unprecedented nine Academy Awards in 1946. It still holds up today and everyone loves it. Me most of all!

And then came the wonderful "The Secret Life of Walter Mitty," another classic, still frequently seen on TV. As I told you before, I actually worked on that film at the same time I was working on "Best Years." I think about doing two movies at once now, and just shake my head. Youth is definitely wasted on the young! In Walter Mitty, Danny Kaye played a man whose mind kept wandering away from his immediate life, and in his imagination he would become heroic, famous, brilliant, -- all the things in real life he wasn't. I played his love interest and while the movie was a huge hit and our acting chemistry was amazingly good, he wasn't, as I've already mentioned, the easiest guy to work with.

It was 1947. World War II was over. The atomic bomb had been dropped out of the Enola Gay straight onto Hiroshima, Japan in the summer of 1945, thus ending the war mess for good. The men and women of the armed forces were home now, and the country was becoming more and more prosperous. Movies were becoming plentiful and so were my parts. I was on a roll. (Or should I say "role." Sorry. Couldn't resist.) I completed "The Secret Life of Walter Mitty" and went on immediately to make "Out of the Blue." I was loaned out for this film by Goldwyn which I thought was pretty chintzy of him. It wasn't that good of a part. It was a film company called Eagle Lyon. The movie was supposed to be a comedy, but really, it wasn't very funny. It was written by some extremely nice people, but sadly, just not awfully amusing.

In that film, I was to play the part of a model who was posing for an artist who lived next door to me. There were two old ladies who would spy on us all the time and would see me posing. I had a dog in that movie too, named "Rabelais." (Named for a famous French poet.) The picture is really kind of cute and Turhan Bey played the part of the artist. We had fun making it. Carole Landis was in it too. The women who played the fussy old ladies were pretty funny, too and did a great job.

In 1947 my five-year contract with Sam Goldwyn was up. I was done. I worried a little about that because he didn't renew it, but within a month, thanks to the help of my agent, I was taken in by Warner Brothers and put under contract, and ended up spending years there, ten or more, making a great many movies, mostly successful ones.

CHAPTER 11

I'd like to talk here about my dear husband Mike O'Shea. As I've already mentioned, he and I met on the set of "Jack London," in which he starred. I had a small role, the one I'd just simply asked for and had gotten, and there I was, working with Mike.

We began to date each other, and the more I saw of him, the more I loved him. I knew he was married but I believed him when he told me his marriage wasn't working out. He was just too honest a man to tell me a lie just so I'd go out with him. Not Mike. It wasn't his style.

I remember when he'd come to dinner at my apartment and how he'd knock on the wall to announce his arrival. We had some wonderful times together and we just became closer and closer.

Finally, after many years of marriage, Mike and his wife divorced and he and I could finally marry. (He'd had a child with his first wife. Her name is Barbara and she is married to someone in the military I think, and they live in the eastern part of the USA.)

We wouldn't have a huge wedding. No. Back then in the movie business, we all worked Saturdays and Sundays without question. We were slaves, I tell you! Maybe willing slaves, but nonetheless, we had no life, or so the producers thought. But it was the life I'd chosen and I was going to make the very best of it, and I never want to give the impression I was unhappy. I never was. I loved my job.

Anyway, Mike and I had a very small wedding on Saturday, July 7th, 1947, a ceremony that sort of squeezed into my work schedule. I was about to begin working on "A Song Is Born" with Danny Kaye and all musicians of note of that era. Steve Cochran was in the movie also, playing the role of a gangster I was supposed to marry. The movie was very funny with a lot of old men playing the professors.

I went back to work on the following Monday after our wedding, so we never really had a honeymoon until we went on the Command Performance trip to London with Alan and Sue Ladd. But we didn't mind really. Mike and I understood the rules of the game.

46

Our wedding cake was a three-tiered affair, beautiful.

My attendants and guests didn't number very many. My friend Adele Jergens was there. We'd appeared together in "Banjo Eyes" with Eddie Cantor years before. I just chatted with her the other day, as a matter of fact! I liked her then and still do. She's a good friend.

Anyway, Vera Ellen, that great dancer and my dear friend, was in attendance too, along with Audrey Kirshbaum who was my Maid of Honor and best friend all my life.

Carmen Miranda was there too! Can you imagine? No, she didn't wear a big fruit thing on her head! She and Mike had been working on a movie and had become pals. She came with her husband. Cathy O'Donnell was there too, and we had a small wedding reception at Mike's house.

My dress was made by Irene Sharaff. She was a wonderful dressmaker and had done so many costumes for me and others, and had done the costuming for numerous Broadway shows. She made beautiful things, even for Goldwyn. She was also under contract with him.

My dress was a soft grey tulle over pink tulle and it was just lovely. I had on a small matching veil, too.

Irene was a fascinating woman. Exotic. She was called "The Black Widow" by everyone. She'd arrive in a small black car and she'd always wear black along with a huge black hat. She made that dress for me on very short notice.

Mike and I had been seeing each other for four years and I guess it was just automatic that we'd marry. (Even though we'd been together all those years, we really didn't know each other very well, surprisingly. I had much to learn about Mike.)

We finally did find a minister to marry us. Too many priests and ministers were reluctant to do the job when we asked them, because Mike had been divorced. Things were very much stricter back then.

Our one-night honeymoon was spent at Mike's house where we'd live. Not very exciting, but after all, I had to work. And I had to soon finish (the still famous) "A Song is Born," with Danny Kaye.

Mike sort of worked, on and off, but he just wasn't aggressive enough. I never pushed at him. It's not my style. Maybe I should have, but I was working and I guess that was enough for him. He was a good man and a very good actor, but his heart wasn't in it. He didn't have the spark or whatever it is actors have. A drive. A yearning. I guess he just simply wasn't passionate about it.

I've said before that I think Mike really wanted to be a police officer, and eventually he became one—on a volunteer basis, and that's when he drove around with Officer Jim Dougherty who has remained my good friend to this day, and I'll tell you more about that later.

I don't think we ever really talked about having children. The issue didn't seem to come up. That may sound surprising, but it's true. It may also sound trite, but we were awfully busy people, planning our lives, working, but finally after about six years of marriage, we started to talk about having a child and thought maybe we ought to just go for it! We tried and tried, but I just didn't get pregnant. Eventually I consulted a doctor and it was discovered that I had an obstruction that disallowed me to get pregnant. I was disappointed, but relieved to finally know the reason for my being unable to conceive.

Surgery was recommended and the doctor told me that it was a generally successful procedure. In 1954, it was. I'll tell you all about Mary later.

CHAPTER 12

It was now 1948 and I'd starred in "Smart Girls Don't Talk," "A Song is Born," (with Goldwyn) and then in 1949 "The Girl From Jones Beach, "Flaxy Martin," "Colorado Territory" (my first western,) "Always Leave them Laughing," "Red Light, and finally "White Heat." 1949 was a pretty busy year for me. Six movies in one year, and I never even took a vacation! I had to work. I felt as if our money was being spent even before I could earn it, and this worried me greatly. Taxes were terrible, and Mike wasn't awfully frugal. I remember how he'd drive our daughter Mary all over Beverly Hills and buy her the most expensive, beautiful dresses. She only wore them once, if that, and it was a terrible waste, but that was how Mike operated with his daughter since her birth in 1954.

"White Heat" was to become another classic and is still seen all the time. I played Jimmy Cagney's wife, only I betray him, and he gets pretty rough with me. Cagney was the consummate actor. He got so into his parts that he found it hard to get out of them when the scene ended. In one scene in "White Heat" he's in a rage and has to choke me to get some information, and I have to weep while he's doing that. I rehearsed and practiced that for a long time. I had my lines down precisely because I knew Jimmy would really be rough with me, and I surely didn't want to have to do any retakes on that scene! When he choked a gal, he really choked! Thankfully, we got it on the first take. This marvelous movie plays all the time, and remains enormously popular. I feel so honored to have been a part of it and have always been surprised about how much African Americans like this film. People are always telling me they can't believe I could be so tough as I was in that movie, but I am an actress for heaven's sake! That's what actors and actresses do! Just because I was in a number of musical comedies doesn't mean I couldn't have a broad range of acting skills.

Anyway, White Heat was a wonderful film, and I'm still hugely shaken when I watch that incredible scene where Cagney's character hears, while eating dinner in the jail at that long table with all the other inmates, that his mother has died. It is powerful, compelling, horrifying and all Cagney! To my utter delight, I would work with him again later.

But after work, back at home, my marriage to Mike was always interesting and never boring. He was a great raconteur, and while an awful lot of his stories were fanciful, he could tell them so well, people were just drawn to him. I can remember journalists and the like coming out to the house to ostensibly interview me and they'd end up gravitating to him. They just got caught up in his wonderful personality, his great story telling. I loved listening to his tales and never tired of them. He was so interesting and I, too, would forget all about me and just concentrate on him. What a personality! Ah, if he'd only pushed himself harder. I think he would have been more successful as an actor if he had. I know he would.

Mike was first discovered in a play in New York City, named "The Eve of St. Mark," a really great play written by Maxwell Anderson. Mike was wonderful in it and got extremely good reviews. He was talked about so much around that city and in the papers that he was offered a contract by producer Hunt Stromberg.

So Mike came to Hollywood expecting in his calm and not so aggressive way, that he'd make it in movies because of the great success of the play and having been "caught" by Stromberg. But Stromberg, as it turned out, could do nothing for him in the long run. Mike did recreate that same role in a movie called "The Eve of St. Mark." He then went on to make movies for Fox Studios and did a few more crummy ones, but they never gave him another good part, and he just wasn't pushing himself enough. That was his main trouble. I knew how to push, to just march up and ask for things, but I was luckier than he. Movie parts just happened to fall in my lap. Mike could not push. He just couldn't and wouldn't do that. It was as if he were unable to. He should have been like Tony Curtis who unabashedly pushed and pushed himself and has remained a big success. If Mike heard of a good part coming up in a film, he never bothered to contact his agent to force the issue, to try to get him that part. My Mike far more enjoyed talking to the workmen on the set in stead of acting. He didn't care about this Hollywood stuff. He just didn't want to actively pursue his acting career the way I did. I guess it could be said that Mike didn't have the burning desire I had or other actors had. I guess they call it "the fire in the belly."

Mike had a very bad habit of telling directors that they could not even "direct traffic on a one way street," which obviously never set too well with those guys. Mike could be kind of abrasive to movie folk! I mean he liked acting, but in his heart I knew he'd always wanted to be a cop. He gave his acting jobs a sort of half-hearted attempt, but police work was his big passion. Whenever Mike was offered a police officer role in the movies or on TV or in a play, he was thrilled. Poor Mike. He really did try to become a police officer. He had a lot of relatives who were, but he was too short and just kept getting turned down. But my Mike wasn't a man to "cry in his beer," although I know it broke his heart when he couldn't be a cop. So even when he discovered he was a naturally gifted actor, he just couldn't force himself to get all that involved. What a pity. What a waste!

It was his love of law enforcement that connected him with Officer James E. Dougherty, a man who is still my friend today.

The story of how those two men got to be friends is a nice one. Mike and I bought a TV series called McGary and his Mouse that unfortunately never really went anywhere. But in order that Mike learn how to "be" a cop, it was suggested he contact someone on the Los Angeles Police Department to ask if he might ride around in a patrol car with him for a few weeks to see how they do their job, to learn the lingo etc. I thought Mike would explode with happiness. I can't remember ever having seen him that happy. The man he was assigned to was Jim Dougherty, a lovable, kind guy, very Irish (perfect for Mike!) and a man who in short order became a dear friend to our family. He would often take our daughter Mary camping with his three daughters Cherrie, Kathy and Mary, and his wife Pat, and sometimes they went even without Pat. We trusted him completely and he gave our daughter some wonderful memories. (Jim loves to tell the story about how our Mary asked him one day up in the hills of California where the bathroom was, and Jim pointed to a bush. Mary, he says, was horrified, but quickly learned how to use those bushes!)

And because of this driving around with Jim, Mike became a "member" of the LAPD on a volunteer basis and I will say he was happiest when he was doing police work with our good friend Jim. And I know Jim gave Mike some jobs to do that as a non-cop he probably should not have been given, but Jim knew he could trust Mike utterly. Mike was a born cop. He just didn't grow tall enough to become one. I wonder if today the LAPD turns down great guys like Mike all for a few inches of growth.

I never tried to talk Mike out of doing that because after all, when I met him, he was starring in "Jack London," so I just assumed he was doing what he loved to do. And in a lot of ways actually he was. Mike truly loved to perform. I mean he couldn't get with two people without putting on a show for them. But it was that other love, the love of police work that I didn't always recognize or see, and he never really made a big deal of it. I just sort of "got it" as our marriage progressed.

Our pal Jim Dougherty had a secret, something he never mentioned to anyone, although most people knew. His first wife had been Marilyn Monroe, only before they were divorced when she was still Norma Jeane Baker. Their courtship and marriage only totaled about five years, but even today, Jim's eyes fill with tears at his loss and the hurt she caused him by dumping him. He's had a wonderful life however, and got the children he wanted with his second wife Pat, and is now very happily married to his third wife Rita. They live in Maine on a beautiful lake and want to spend the rest of their lives there. But they have family out in California and so I get to see Jim and Rita when they come out. Incidentally, Jim wrote a book about his years with Norma Jeane and it's called "To Norma Jeane with Love, Jimmie." A sad, sweet story, and yes, Jimmie will plug my book, too!

Jim and Mike became the dearest of friends. Rita remembers Mike as being such a generous man. She recalls how there would always be a small gift from him awaiting her on her dinner plate when they went to restaurants together. Mike was a great gift giver—too great really. His wild generosity caused us no small amount of problems.

Mike also had one big secret. He wasn't Irish. Never was. Michael O'Shea was French, his mother was French-Canadian and his father was from Scotland. Mike's stepfather was, at least, Irish, but oh, how Mike also yearned to be Irish, and I think his step-father helped him along in that secret wish. So much so in fact, that he just simply became Irish! After all, he looked it, acted like it and loved the Irish. So Mike invented a birthday—you guessed it, St. Patrick's Day, said he was born in New York City, (he was not) and added an O to his family name which was Shay or Chez or Shea. He invented family members from Ireland, invented Irish ancestry, and he gradually, simply just became Irish. And I'll tell you this---I think the Irish would forgive him this little indiscretion. He well represented his "mother land," and I think if someone wants to be something badly enough, well then he can be that very thing. Frankly, I think Mike was more Irish than most Irish people are, and as far as the Irish are concerned after all, everyone's Irish! And so that was my Mike's little secret.

CHAPTER 13

I so well remember when I eventually went to Warner Brothers, I was immediately able to get the famous director Raoul Walsh on my side. That man wanted to put me in every movie he ever made! He loved me!

He tested me for "Colorado Territory" playing against Rock Hudson. Alas, Rock was not to be in that movie. At that point, he was just feeding me lines. Who knew this big guy saying lines back to me would one day become such a gigantic star? I'd like to say that I "had a feeling" about him, but I didn't. However it is always amazing to me how the star thing happens, and it sure happened to him!

But I so clearly remember when Rock was being considered for a part, that he had a rather bad attitude about commitment. Raoul had him under contract, hoping he'd become a big star, which of course he did. But Rock just didn't get it. He would wander onto the set around noon, after the rest of us had been working since 6 AM, and Raoul would say "Rock, you have to get on the set and work with the cowboys at dawn. You do not just decide to show up at noon or one o/clock." I guess Rock just didn't enjoy being a tough guy in any role—gangster or cowboy. He would show up finally on the set, and then just goof around. He liked to play! He was just a huge kid. Raoul would scold him, but Rock would just pour on that gigantic, charming grin routine and all would be forgiven---until the next time. I had to play a half-Indian whose name would be Colorado Carson, a kind of remote role for me. They darkened my naturally blonde hair and put on very dark make-up and amazingly enough, I got the part! I'm not kidding when I say Raoul loved me!

We made that film out in New Mexico and I had a ball doing it. The hills were wonderful; dark red, breathtaking. It was just plain marvelous working there. I'd always loved being in the outdoors, so doing this film was a happy situation for me. I rode horses in that movie, although a double was used mostly, and even though Mike and I owned horses, I really disliked them then and dislike them now! They can hurt you, you know! Everyone always says how marvelous those big animals are. Well, I don't think they're so marvelous. They're huge and temperamental and tricky. And they smell, too. Give me a dog any day of the year over a horse!

I recall one way Raoul would inspire us to do a scene. He'd invent some idea for us to think about. For example, if we were supposed to run away fast, he'd say "You're very, very hot and thirsty, and you've just heard that free beer is being served just around that corner." I was so happy to have gotten that part. I truly wanted it and enjoyed it so much.

The wonderful, sweet Joel MacRae was in that movie too. Joel had been a near neighbor of ours, Mike's and mine, when we built our home in Thousand Oaks and were the only house on the block. I recall his coming to our door with his son Peter to welcome us when we moved in. What a nice man Joel was. He was exactly as he appeared in his films—gentle, and kind and funny. Very handsome! A sweet, dear man. I liked him very much. (Joel knew his wife would never invite me over for tea to welcome me to the neighborhood because she was snobbish, withdrawn and jealous of his leading ladies, so he came himself. And that was fine with me.)

"Colorado Territory," my first outdoor film and first Western, (Joel and I died in the end, guns a-blazin'!) it had been filmed in black and white, and I was recently delighted to see a colorized version of it on television. I know people are in an uproar about that new process, but not I! I think it's marvelous, wonderful. Of course certain films should never be colorized, such as, for example, "A Streetcar Named Desire." That film needs its dark look, its sadness and even morbidity. "High Noon" would not have had the same emotion and feel to it had it been in color. I understand that some films just should be left in black and white, but the majority of them look wonderful in color. It's like a whole new movie. I used to hate seeing myself in black and white and I yearned for the filmgoers to be able to see the colors I was seeing. Well, I guess it's obvious that I'm crazy about colorization. Now, because of this wonderful new artform, people can see those New Mexico hills and mountains as I saw them in "Colorado Territory," cloaked in the most beautiful of colors—purples, greens, blues, soft reds and oranges. I think it's just great that certain films are being magically transformed into color. Heck, if people don't like it, they can always push the color buttons on their TV sets or their remotes to off and there it'll be, black and white again! No problem. I sure wish people wouldn't be so adamantly against colorization. I mean it allows us to see how things really were, what colors we wore. And those of us in the business who are still alive can tell the colorization people what we wore and what all the colors were. While I realize that some films just look and play better in black and white, colorizing of films makes them much more realistic, I think, and I love it.

54

My next film after "Colorado Territory" was "Always Leave them Laughing" in 1949, starring Milton Berle, a really overblown comedy. But Uncle Miltie was a big TV star and so the studios were anxious to get him into their films, to bring in the ticket sales. I got to do some dancing in that film, some with Bert Lahr, who was in that movie too. He was a really nice guy. Berle was, and remains, manic! It really wasn't and still isn't my favorite film, and I remember telling the producers that I'd do the part if they'd let me sing and dance and do musicals in the future, and in fact, later on they did. It was what I most wanted to do in show business. I did so love to dance! Their word was their bond and that's what I believed. I eventually began to be able to follow my dearest dream---to dance in films! Well, at least six of them. They kept offering me dramatic roles, and I learned early on that if you want to stay alive in show business, you'd better know how to do everything and to say yes as often as you can. Sometimes, to my sadness, a few people don't remember my dancing but do remember my dramatic roles. That's fine. But I sure wish I could have danced in many more films.

After "Always Leave Them Laughing," came "Red Light" and "White Heat," as mentioned above, and even though I loved making those films, I can't stress it enough that I adored making the musicals. I feel no shame in that! I loved doing them and still love watching them, and could watch them over and over and never get bored. Aunt Alice really gave me such a good background that dancing and singing in those films just came very naturally to me. My childhood training was perfect and really helped to keep my legs up and going until I couldn't dance anymore.

My next role was "The Girl From Jones Beach," and even though I again didn't dance, as I've stated before, dancing came naturally to me, although I did take lessons all along the way. Before each musical, I was assigned a dance instructor as were all the other cast members who had to dance in that particular film, and we did rehearse and rehearse to exhaustion! Time was money (still is!) and directors weren't fond of people who missed steps causing the dance scene to be re-shot. It was better for everyone involved if we had it nailed down from the beginning of the filming to the end.

It always took about six weeks to get all the rehearsals done, to get the legs in shape. The best advice I can give to dancers today is to never stop dancing. If you dance for movies, (or today for TV and even for commercials,) it's best to keep your body and legs constantly ready, by dancing and dancing. This isn't always so easy when one has a life! Even movie stars have responsibilities and obligations and can't always fit time in for practice, but we must. I often read how people who today make their livings by dancing, go to work out in gyms all the time. That's a wonderful idea. It keeps the body toned for when they have to dance on stage or in front of a camera.

And barre work! Every single day. Ballet dancers in particular, but all of us dancers did endless barre work. Learning numbers was fun, but barre work? Never! Ah but dancing! Dancing is the most fun thing anybody can ever do! It's never a chore. Really, it is absolutely never a chore!

Unfortunately, I never got a chance to meet or dance with Gene Kelly or Fred Astaire because they were in different studios. But I did know an awful lot of dancers in the industry, and one of the best in the business, of course, was my dear friend Gene Nelson with whom I appeared in "She's Working Her Way Through College" and "She's Back On Broadway." I starred again with Gene in "Painting The Clouds With Sunshine." What a great guy, a fabulous athlete, good man and what a dancer! Powerful, sexy, emotional. What a force. If you ever want to see one of the finest, most athletic, beautifully timed dance sequences ever done in film, watch Gene Nelson in the college gym scene from "She's Working Her Way Through College." He is all muscle, no strain, and it is a classic, classy piece of work. I understand that Gene's son has put together all of his father's dance sequences into one film. I haven't seen it, but I do look forward to watching it one day, so if you ever hear of its being on TV, don't miss it. Gene was the very, very best. I can't say enough about that man and his talent.

I remember loving to watch any dance number between Gene Kelly and Cyd Charisse, for example. Now that was dancing! Cyd was a disciplined and fabulous dancer, and had the most beautiful, long legs.

And my dear old friend, Vera Ellen. Oh, could she dance. What energy! That woman could do tap on the points of her ballet slippers. She was amazing. As I told you, she was one of the witnesses at my wedding to Mike.

Take Margot Fontane. What a magnificent dancer. She danced for decades, and went on far longer than most, well into her sixties. Remember her magical, fabulous ballet partnering with Rudolf Nureyev? I so admired her. She was just beyond good. Ballet dancers have to work every single day and do at least an hour on the barre or they'll lose their muscles. They dance! Every single day, dancers like Margot dance, and do not just do the marking. ("Marking" means to not dance full-out. Marking is doing a slight rendering of the number to perhaps conserve strength, and is largely doing the dance more in the mind.)

Being a ballerina is a slave life. I never got into much ballet, but when I did, it was hard, hard work. But I'll state here that dancing every day will make old age easier to endure. At this writing, I'm eighty years old and I still

56

get around pretty easily and don't have to hang onto people when I walk and I don't have to use a cane or a walker. I remember tripping over one of our dogs—they're Border Terriers and the light of my life—while walking down our stairs, but I didn't get hurt because I knew how to fall from my dancing years. Dancing has been very good to me.

I remember Juliet Prowse. Oh, what a dancer! Marvelous. And another woman I admire is Shirley MacLaine. She does everything, and could she ever dance. Everything Shirley does she makes her own. She is just terrific, so personable and nice. I like her tremendously, although I think more of her dancing than her acting. But she can be outrageous!

I guess maybe I really can't enjoy movies the way "civilians" can, having been in the business for so long. I can always "see" what actors are up to when they're trying to portray an elderly person or something other than what they are in real life. I mean I do enjoy films, but the things that go over a viewer's head don't go over mine because I know the tricks. And I can always tell when things are being faked a bit too much.

I understand that it's recommended that actors today learn how to do everything in the business so that when "the call" comes and they're asked if they can do some certain kind of performance, they can in all honesty say "yes, I can do that." Back in my day not all actors and actresses (yes I like to say "actress" instead of lumping everyone as "actor." Anyway--) back in my day if all you really cared about was being a dramatic actress or actor, then you just let it be known that you couldn't or wouldn't do singing and dancing. But many stars back then did learn to do a lot of different things because even then there was so much competition it was important for actors and actresses to have at least some knowledge about how to perform other forms of entertainment.

It seems to me that many actors in musicals have made the transition to serious acting rather well, but it wasn't always true in the reverse. Fred Astaire did it. He became a very good dramatic actor and did one of his best jobs in that famous and scary movie "On The Beach." John Travolta is a good example of a man's becoming a serious dancer in films after a career in dramatic (or comedic) acting. So I guess it can be done. It's just not the norm.

In many interviews, I'm asked which form of film entertainment I most enjoyed, and of course the answer is, obviously, the musicals. But I did an awful lot of serious or dramatic acting too and can state here that I find it far more difficult and stressful to do dramatic over musical films. It's very hard—--hard on your body and your mind. You have to pull all the anger out of you for an angry scene, all the sadness in a sad scene. That takes its toll on your body and mind, just like anger in real life does. It just takes it all out of you. It burns you up.

I also want to say that I think something good is taken out of you when you have to be mean or angry or sad over and over in a movie. When I've had to do powerful scenes in a movie where I was to be angry, furious etc., I'd have to just walk away from it all and sit for an hour and rest to get things back in their proper balance again. Honestly, dramatic acting can take a lot out of a person.

As for crying. Well, I'm not the type who ever really cries much, so that didn't come all that easily to me. Some actors force themselves to think of something dreadfully sad in their lives and that makes them cry. Not I. Some actresses can weep copiously at the drop of a hat. When I had to do a crying scene, I occasionally had to have someone put those glycerin drops in my eyes, and don't think they don't burn because oh, they do! And today everyone knows that this little trick is used. It's not that I'm spilling the beans about a big Hollywood secret. All people in our business need the occasional little assistance now and again! But I think I could carry the crying scenes off pretty well. When I watch myself cry on screen, it looks pretty believable.

And speaking of crying on cue; June Allyson is the best at that. She was and remains a good friend of mine and we talk on the phone frequently. I'll discuss the cruise part of my life in later pages, but June and I went on a number of very fancy cruises together, the kind of cruise where you travel first class and all they want is one big interview with you and any or all guests who want to attend. The cruise people always want we old stars to mingle with the passengers every day. Well I wasn't much keen on talking to everyone on shipboard, but June always did. She's great like that. Anyway, she was so ingenuous, such a charming actress and was so incredibly popular. All those wonderful films she made with Jimmy Stewart, all her singing and dancing. She also could do it all and do it well—drama, and musical comedies. I remember well when she was appearing in "No, No, Nanette" in San Francisco and she was getting sick of it and wanted to stop doing the show, so they asked me to step in for her. I did it happily. I had to go up there to watch Junie perform, to learn everything she did, and it was just sheer pleasure! She was and is just so professional and it made me admire her even more. What a talent! She was always so darling. Cute without being sickening. (And as a small "aside," I'll tell here how June used to stick her chewing gum on the wall just before she went on stage, and after many performances there were just dozens of pieces of chewed June Allyson gum going up and down the staircase to the stage! She was very funny.)

And cry? Oh, June was a champion at it! Could turn 'em on in an instant. I like her so much. June Allyson lives north of me with her husband, and is happily married. She is the genuine article—a real What You See Is What You Get kind of person. She's very high on my list of people I like and admire.

There are some actresses who really do make me awfully uncomfortable when they have to cry in a scene, because even with gallons of glycerin and all those sobbing noises and their scrunched up faces, it is just awful and completely unbelievable.

Margaret O'Brien was a champ at crying too, especially as a child actress. She could bring everyone to tears when she wept on screen. Margaret is a good friend and I like her enormously. She was just simply excellent on screen, and everyone will always remember her.

I've often been asked which actors and actresses I admire most, and the answer is very clear to me. The actors and actresses I admire above all others are the ones who moved into appropriate roles as they aged. You never saw Burt Lancaster trying to do his swashbuckling stuff when he got into his seventies. Bette Davis tried to hold it together for maybe too many years and then finally gave in and began to act her age. "Whatever Happened to Baby Jane" was a great role for her and she let herself look really old, and even grotesque in it. Goldie Hawn is still able to be cute, but she's fifty something now and really doesn't have an awful lot of time left to do that. I hope she either disappears or accepts roles where she can act the age she really is. I mean "Laugh-In" is long gone! But I do admire her because she's a wonderful dancer and actress. She's a pleasure to watch work, and definitely worth her weight!

Want to know who my favorite actor is today? Well, there are two. The first is Charles Bronson! Surprised? The reasons are simple. For one, he shows all that weathering in his face. The man's got "it!" Look what he's done in his career. He began as an extra and became the star of the world! I do admire him very much.

The second one I admire very much is the endlessly great Walter Matthau. Is there another actor anywhere who could handle all roles with such ease and grace and humor? He was glorious no matter what role he took on, but his best work of course, was humor. He is a joy forever! I hope he and his dear friend Jack Lemmon are having a fabulous time together in heaven. They were indeed the odd couple but loved one another madly and dearly. It showed on the screen when they worked together.

I always loved Bette Davis's work. She was good at every single thing she did. She seemed to be able to do nothing wrong in her films. We weren't friends, but we'd appear at functions together, sometimes with my sitting right next to her, and guess what? She would never say a single word to me. It was just so weird! But I probably wouldn't have talked to her anyway because she was so feisty and mean! So I'd just sit there. That woman couldn't even say hello or good evening. She was one rude person, but I suppose she thought she was Hollywood royalty or something, and so didn't really have to bother to speak to common folk like me.

I remember once when Look magazine wanted to take a picture for one of their covers, and they chose Ann Blyth, Bette Davis and me to pose together. We all had to show up at this place where we could sit for the picture. Well, I saw Anne at first and we chatted a long time (she is just so nice and still incredibly beautiful) and then Bette swept in. She began to talk to Ward Bond who also happened to be there for another photograph. Bette never spoke a word to either Anne or me. It was awful! We all sat in our places so we could do the picture and I decided to smile. At that point I didn't really give a hoot if La Davis would approve or not. The cover turned out to be OK, I guess. I am certain Bette thought she was the Queen of Hollywood and better than everyone, so regarded everyone else on earth as riffraff, which apparently she thought Ann and I were! There was Bette Davis and there was the rest of humanity. That day with her was one dreadful experience.

But still, I have to admit that Davis was a remarkable and versatile actress and there was really nothing, save maybe roles in musicals, that she was not capable of attacking and doing with a flourish and to perfection. And I do remember reading in one of her autobiographies that she told someone that "Virginia Mayo should have done that role in that movie, and not me. Better for her than for me." I don't remember the movie of which she spoke, but it was flattering, considering she couldn't ever be bothered to speak to me. However, to give credit where it's due, at the American Cinema Foundation Awards in 1988, she did say that I should have won an Oscar for my performance in The Best Years of Our Lives.

It was so nice for me to have seen Ann Blyth that day. She's one who made the transition from singing to dramatic acting very well, and had the good sense to back away from it all when she got older. Remember her playing Joan Crawford's terrible daughter in "Mildred Pierce?" She was excellent in that, and didn't sing a note. She married Dennis Day's brother who's a physician, and I do like her a lot.

I never met Joan Crawford, but occasionally she'd come onto a set where I was working where she'd sit and knit—she was forever knitting something—I guess hoping the male star of my movie would come out to say hello to her. Crawford did have a thing for the men! And, like her archenemy Bette Davis, she also couldn't be bothered to say hello to me. Very snooty woman. She and Bette were really wonderful in "Whatever Happened to Baby Jane," although Bette stole that movie from her for certain. I wonder how they got along on the set. Not well, I hear, but they really were fabulous in that.

Sadly Crawford ended her career making horrible movies, sort of science-fictiony. That happens to a lot of actors at the end of their careers. They end up making these dreadful films, but they have to eat too, and pay the rent, so I guess they had to do what they had to do. Claude Rains is a very good example of that. What a wonderful actor he was, and that voice! Oh my. His final movies were an embarrassment. Same thing happened to Peter Lorre and hundreds of other famous and good actors. Well, it happens. When I see those movies, I admire the acting ability of those "fallen stars" but am so saddened that they've had to resort to that.

But as I think about that, why did they do it? They'd had their fame. They'd had their time in the sun. And most of them could easily pay the rent and had loads of money. I don't know. Perhaps they thought if they just kept their faces out there for people to see that they'd get the old glory back somehow. I guess they had this compulsive need to work, and that's deeply saddening. Being famous is like a drug, I suppose, and for some, the addiction is just too much and they have to keep "using." And maybe they thought that if they just kept on plugging away in movies, any kinds of movies, someone would rediscover them and they'd have their glory back, the old days, the adoration and money, cars, mansions, pools, playmates. It's awfully, dreadfully sad when that all happens to people in our business.

I never had that particular pull. I've been OK with all phases of my life and haven't had this terrible yearning to get back into the Golden Years of Hollywood. I mean, let's get real. They're over for good. I'd love to see those old types of films come back, the crazy, beautiful wonderful musical comedies, but they won't. And even if they did, I think the American public is so skeptical now and so used to violence and sex that they'd lose interest very fast. What a tragedy. Sure those movies didn't make much sense and sure they didn't have heavy messages, but for a couple of hours in that theater, people could watch and applaud and laugh and cry and sing along and tap their feet, and when they left that theater, they were happier people. I know it.

Oh now look. I know it's unrealistic, by today's standards, to "believe" scenes where extras wandering around in the background can suddenly all burst into song and dance numbers knowing every single step perfectly. I know it's impossible to imagine that glamorous women in a sleep scene would awaken from dreamland and leap from bed in a perfect peignoir with every hair in place and loads of make-up on their faces. But it's a matter of "suspending our disbeliefs." It was fun. It wasn't real, but who cared? And furthermore, have you ever seen people without make-up in a film? They vanish! They just have a blank face. So we wore make-up! Sometimes tons! We wanted to be seen, to have all of our facial characteristics seen! We should feel ashamed for doing that? I'm not. I wasn't.

Besides, it was no picnic to get up while it was still dark and sit in a make-up chair getting made up for the film. We got up so early to do our work, and the make-up people had to get up early too. There was a lot of pressure on them to make us look perfect, and the make-up had to be consistent. I mean, if we were filming a scene on one day and a similar scene was scheduled for the next day and we had to look exactly the same, it was up to the make-up people to make that happen, down to every strand of hair looking exactly as it had looked the day before. That's a real art form!

One of my favorite make-up men was Henry Vilardo who is now a lawyer. Make-up people not only have to put the stuff onto our faces and bodies, but they had to hang around the sets all day to do touch-ups. I mean under those hot lights the make-up would melt off! Make-up and fittings— oh, they took forever.

Getting up early and working wasn't always so much fun, but one got into a routine and made it happen. It wasn't always easy, but we did it and I'm glad. I never look back on any part of my show business career and complain about it. It was all just simply marvelous!

And, by the way, for what it's worth, I was never, ever fired from a film. That would have been unthinkable. When I signed on to do a job, the job would get done.

But, those wonderful old films, they simply lifted people's hearts. No, they didn't carry any heavy societal message, and yes, maybe they made some women feel insecure because they didn't sing and dance and look perfect at dawn, but in the main, those movies provided entertainment, and that was their only goal. We wanted to entertain people, to make them feel good, to give them a laugh or have them think about things, or to even leave the theater humming those new tunes. It was done just for the joy! Just for the joy.

CHAPTER 14

I had the chance to work with the gentle and sweet Alan Ladd in a couple of films, and we had wonderful time acting together.

I really loved that man. There wasn't anyone nicer in Hollywood and we became good friends. The rumor is that he killed himself, and I've always worried about the fact that maybe if I'd just called him in Palm Springs where he lived, maybe if I'd just done that, he wouldn't have shot himself. I'll never know, but it will haunt me. His wife Sue died shortly after that, too. It was just too sad and awful.

I remember his being in a film with George Peppard where Alan played a has-been actor, and it was so pathetic, like his real life, and it was terrible and awful, although he gave a fabulous performance. He'd just lost it, lost his verve. He was unsure of himself then because he was unsure of himself always. The Hollywood people would criticize him for not having any talent. No talent? Then why did he appear in so many films? Why did they make so much money from him? These stories spread around and they always get back to the actors, and for a man as sensitive and kind as Alan was---well, those stories must have hurt him horribly, just so much.

Alan was the only actor back then who got on the cover of magazines because he had that beautiful face. And one vision of his face really still haunts me to this very day and is even hard to talk about. He and I were starring in "The Iron Mistress" in 1952 and his character was in love with my character. In that picture, Alan was always after me to marry him, but I wouldn't because I was such a snob. I was wealthy and he wasn't. He wasn't at my social level. Oh, I was such a phony woman. However, in the film I at one point had promised I'd go away with him, but obviously had changed my mind.

In this particular scene, I was getting into my carriage and had my umbrella and he came over to me and said hello. We spoke, and I then introduced him to my husband. He didn't know I had married. He looked up at me and I have never, ever seen such an expression on a man. He was so hurt. It was terrible. He looked at me as if to say "Why? Why did you marry him? You promised you'd marry me." Oh it was a terrible expression.

I'll never forget it. Now that's acting. I mean if that expression on his face could have affected me, a fellow actor, then it must have come across to the audience that way too. He was a marvel, and I miss him dreadfully.

Mike and I traveled across the ocean with Alan and Sue Ladd because we were asked to do a Royal Command Performance in London for the Queen. Alan was so friendly to us during that voyage. When we arrived we knew we had to do a scene on a stage for the Queen, and Alan suddenly, on the trip, became so frightened about what was coming, so timid, that Mike decided the best thing to do would be to give him some pointers as we traveled, so that by the time we arrived, he'd be all set to perform. Don't forget, Mike got his start working on stage to a live audience, so he really was in a position to help Alan. And, Mike really did help Alan a lot, so when the time came for our "command performance" on stage in front of the Queen and all that royalty, he did quite well. And during the photo sessions, Mike would always push Alan forward so he'd look taller. Mike was sweet that way. I know Alan knew, and I know he loved Mike for doing that.

Alan Ladd's wife Sue had gotten him into the business at the start and made sure he got all those starring roles, but he was so shy and sweet that I think in reality he really never wanted to be an actor. She would always push Alan into getting into crowds to sign autographs, which he was sort of reluctant to do, but he did it because she told him it was important for his career. But oh, how he hated to do that. He was so shy.

We had to do a comedy skit for the Royalty when we were there. The British love slapstick, you know, and comedy too, so we did it and did it pretty well. I remember we had to be given some instruction on how to behave when we met the Royals. We had to go through a crash course on how to not speak until spoken to, to curtsy and all that. When I met the Prince of Wales I curtsied very low and he said, "What is that you have in your hair?" (I'd sprinkled gold glitter in my hair that night for the performance.) I grinned at him and said "well, it's gold dust!" And he said "My! You Americans are richer than I'd thought!"

I so clearly remember that night standing in line out in the lobby after the show to meet the Royals. I stood next to John Mills. We were lined up alphabetically, and Mayo came before Mills. It made me feel odd to be coming before him, but the rule was alphabetical and that was that! No one messed with the Rules of Royalty! But it was lovely, meeting that great, famous actor. John Mills was such a gentleman.

Patricia Neal was along on that trip too, and we became good friends and remained so. She was wonderful, one of the best actresses in the business, if you ask me. There wasn't much she couldn't do in front of a camera. I even think she was more talented than Bette Davis in a lot of ways. Remember that horrible stroke Pat had? She recovered from that, but oh, the struggle, and she went on a big campaign to enlighten people about strokes and how to cope if you have one, and how to avoid getting them. She visited hospitals and everything. That stroke really ruined her life. She would have gone on to do great things in film. She finally did marry but had awful things happen to her during that period of her life. I admire her enormously. And don't forget that she was grieving terribly over her broken romance with Gary Cooper during that trip. Oh, she was and is some woman! A truly wonderful lady.

I remember Joan Caulfield being on that ship too. She was so often mistaken for me and truly we did look alike. I don't know why we were never cast as sisters in a movie, but if we had, it would have been very believable.

CHAPTER 15

"South Sea Woman" came next for me. It was a comedy with Burt Lancaster again, and that big, tall ex-baseball player, Chuck Connors. Remember him? He got really famous doing a weekly TV show called "The Rifleman." He was about six six, and this was his first picture. Oh my, he was tall! My neck would really ache when I had to look up at him from close range. The man could give you vertigo!

Unfortunately, even though it was supposed to be a comedy, no one actually realized that, if you can believe it. In one scene I remember, we were in Chinese waters, and got dumped into them, as I remember, and our costumes shrunk and oh boy, they were just funny looking, too tight and too short and embarrassing and just awful!

Burt liked to direct Chuck Connors, and he did it all during the picture. The director, Arthur Lubin, didn't seem to mind which I recall surprised me somewhat. Directors typically can be very temperamental people, not liking actors to invade their turfs! But Burt had his way, and Chuck was grateful, and Arthur let it go.

CHAPTER 16

My daughter Mary actually has had a brief but important acting "career." She starred with me, well actually she was inside me in "Devil's Canyon" in 1953, although no one knew. Even when I watch that film today I can't see any bulges. I carried Mary throughout that movie and even rode horseback a little, although a double was mostly used.

Soon it was time for me to become a mother. I had one more appointment with the doctor before the expected time of delivery. But before the actual birth, I was X-rayed and it was discovered to our concern that Mary would be a breech baby. There was no hope of natural childbirth for me. Mike was so worried, but I was given a Cesarean and there she was, our beautiful little Mary. We were finally a real family.

After I got home with Mary, I was startled to hear Mike tell me he didn't want anyone to know about the Cesarean delivery, or about the difficulties of the birth. Of all people, he, my husband, didn't want the subject brought up. For reasons I still can't fathom, back in those days, to be married, pregnant or a parent meant you were no longer sexy, and I guess Mike bought into all that. The audiences, he argued with me, would be grossed out at the thought of my beautiful body having that scar. I reluctantly went along with his wishes, but I wish he hadn't thought like that. It just isn't right, after all, and women shouldn't always have to project some sort of virginal aura. It's silly. Well, maybe Mike thought that way because of the fact that I was the main breadwinner in our family and he wanted me to be careful of that situation and to protect that part of our lives. So he perhaps thought I might lose my popularity by becoming "lessened" since I was married and a mother, and what's worse, a mother with a big scar! The potential of losing my popularity may have scared him. Things were very different then. Today's actors and actresses can have huge families and still be big box office draws, and still be very sexy. Heck, they don't even have to be married and still they can have it all. It's easier now. It surely is.

Mary was a good-sized baby, seven pounds three ounces, and she immediately became the light of our lives. I hadn't known I could fall in love with a little baby the way I did with Mary, but I did. I hadn't been around babies very much, and just had no idea the wonderful good feelings having a baby could give a woman. Motherly. Nurturing. It was good.

But, I had to go back to work in six week. Six weeks! My baby was still brand new! It was unheard of back then for a mother to leave her child at such a young age. Oh I know there were mothers back then who had huge families and farms to run, even businesses, and they went back to work almost immediately, but the general rule was that new mothers rested for a long time in the hospital and then again at home, if that was possible. And I could not do that. I had to work. Money was always a consideration, and besides, Mike could stay home with Mary. And we had help, too.

And I guess today young or new mothers go back to work fairly soon after delivering. But back when I had Mary, even if you'd had a baby naturally, you were kept in the hospital for a long time and looked after. I understand the positives and negatives of all that, but I do wish I'd had the luxury of staying home and sleeping and resting. I had to, so badly, but I could not. I simply was not healed up yet after six weeks and I felt so terribly sore.

I had contractual obligations, so reluctantly went back to work to star with Rex Harrison in "King Richard and the Crusaders." Oh, I hurt so much. It was terribly difficult for me to do that movie, very hard on my still tender incision, and of course, extremely hard for me to leave my new baby every day.

In the first scene of that movie, I remember Rex had to serenade me as he strolled around playing a lyre, singing. Laaaa laaaaa daaaa daaaa. I had to sit on a chair listening to him, enraptured. Oh, how that hurt too!

During many, many interviews over the years I've been asked if I ever wanted more children with Mike. No. I did not. Heck, I'm no breeder! I'd had so much trouble having Mary that we decided one was enough for us. Mike always said that Mary was enough children for him! He was awfully happy with her.

In some short time after Mary's birth, Mike amazingly began work on a TV show called "It's A Great Life," on which he worked for three years straight. And I'll tell you here about my Mike's nervous breakdown because of his endlessly hard work on that show. Back then, the work schedule for TV actors can only be described as brutal. Mike did two shows a week for months and months for a full three years, and it was wearing him down. Mike always put 150% into everything he did, and finally, he just could not go on any longer. He would tell me that he couldn't do it any longer, that he was just running dry. He began to stay in bed. Mike became unable to function.

68

Mike had to be hospitalized. He was simply out of control and there's no other way to say it. But fortunately for all of us and thank God, while Mike was in the hospital, they discovered that he had an aneurysm. It was operated on successfully, but that piece of news didn't exactly thrill Mike, and he dreaded the operation. After it was over, I'm sorry to say, he became even more depressed.

But still, even with his grueling schedule, Mike was able to be home with Mary a lot. He adored her. She was his reason to live. Now he had a real purpose in life; to care for Mary when he could, even though we did have nannies for her for when we both had to be away. Also, when he was home, Mike could care for the buildings, land, horses and dogs on our "ranch." I was eager, every night, to get home to my family, my baby, where I could take over the role of mother. I so enjoyed that. Mary looked so much like her father back then, and still does today, all these years later. She has large blue/green eyes, strawberry blond hair, and Mike's big grin. She is like her father in so many ways. I look at her and see Mike every day of my life. Mary also has Mike's kindness and sense of fun. She has a great many friends, just as he did, and is a good parent to her children as her father was to her.

We both adored our beautiful baby Mary. But to put a really fine point on it, I adored her but Mike was besotted with her! Mary was the very best thing that had ever happened to him. He could not stay away from her, and was eager to be "Mr. Mom" whenever he could stay home and be with her, although that was not a title back then. My husband was a good actor, but he just didn't know how to nor did he want to, particularly sell himself. Now that Mary was with us, he really seemed to lose whatever interest in acting he had left. Our child was his life.

When she got older and wasn't in school, Mike took Mary with him everywhere in his small, beautiful gull-wing Mercedes. Oh how he loved that car! I wish I still had it. I have so many photos of them together, doing things, going places. Mike worshipped his beautiful Mary Catherine, and to see them together was to know that she adored him, too.

The two of them would speed all over Beverly Hills and have lunch together, most often at Nate and Al's, a great Deli and one of their favorite spots on earth. I think Mike even had his own parking spot at the side of the restaurant! He'd buy Mary so many beautiful clothes to wear, now that she was out of Catholic school and didn't have to wear those uniforms any longer. Oh, how she'd hated them!

When I think back, I really do think Mary thrived on the life we gave to her. I remember how she'd sit on a chest at the side of my big bedroom and watch me put on make-up. I know she wanted me to stay home with her all the time, but it wasn't possible. I'll easily admit that I loved my career and was proud of my accomplishments and really never entertained the idea of quitting, but I did feel a lot of guilt about having to have left her so often, and for such long periods of time while I went off on location to make movies. She told me a few years ago that she would sometimes, when she was little, try to hide in my suitcases so I'd take her along with me. That made us both feel sad, but Mike at least was there for her.

I do recall one sadistic nanny. Rosalind Russell had recommended her to me. This woman took it upon herself to discipline Mary in ways I found unacceptable. One time my daughter had used some language this woman disapproved of, so she took my little girl and washed out her mouth with soap. When Mary told me that, I not only believed her, I was livid and fired that woman on the spot. It was not for her to punish our child. It was up to us to decide what was appropriate language and what was not. It was up to us to decide what was appropriate punishment and what was not. And it was up to this woman to tell us about Mary's misbehavings so that we, not she, could react in the correct manner for our child as we saw fit. That was abuse, and it left Mary with some very bad memories too, which bothers me to this day. That nanny had come straight from Ireland, and if that's what they did or do with their kids over there, then fine, (no, it's not,) but she had no right to do that to my little girl. She made Mary cry. She hurt and embarrassed her. Well, she didn't last more than an hour after I came home and discovered that! She was gone and that was that. I protected my child and we got another nanny immediately, and she turned out to be very acceptable.

Our Mary grew and flourished. She had playmates and a good life. We put her in Catholic school where she did fairly well and where she continued going until the tenth grade. She then went to Thousand Oaks High school from which she graduated in 1971.

I guess everything worked out all right because today, I live with Mary and her husband Kent and their three sons, my darling grandchildren, Lucas, Evan and Dillon, in the big Spanish style home I built with Mike. We have a good life together and take care of each other.

I have so much more to tell you about Mary and her life and what she did, about her very successful marriage to Kent (they were so young when they married) and the other successes in her life. And I will talk about these things as I go along.

But all of these things, Mike's tearing about buying Mary clothing and gas for the car (to say nothing of the repairs for it—gull-wing Mercedes are expensive to repair) cost us a great deal of money. Because I knew I'd have to be away a lot, and perhaps Mike too sometimes, we really had to have a good-sized staff to run our home, and of course, these people had to be paid. They weren't going to work for the love of it, after all.

On our ranch, we had housekeepers and gardeners, and a man who served as a driver or butler, which was all very nice because we never had to cook or clean or go to the market—or do anything much at all that comes with owning a home with land to groom, and people and animals to feed and care for. On the plus side though, all these good people who worked for us freed me up to be able to pursue my acting jobs, in the movies and later on in plays.

But Mike and I finally began to notice that all of our paychecks were going to pay the people on our staff, so we had to make a decision to get rid of at least two of them. We kept one woman who was very nice. She cooked and cleaned for us and did a great job. Her name was Mrs. Ingrham.

CHAPTER 17

Mike was toiling in his new TV Show, "It's A Great Life." In those early days of "sitcoms" the work was extremely hard and the TV seasons for a show were a great deal longer than they are now. Today you see repeats of the new shows that had begun in late September sometimes a couple of weeks after the first show of the season. (Are the actors off on vacation then or something? I don't understand that.) And they finish the year out in early May, so they work really less than 8 months a year. Oh I know they have to be freed up for other things, but we as viewers get only a few new shows to watch and then have to look at reruns. And of course those TV actors and actresses today get paid like professional athletes who also get paid far too much for what they do. I guess I have a problem with all of this. I know the times have changed, but I think about how hard we all worked back then, getting all these things started, you know, kind of like trailblazers for this industry, and I see how "easy" everyone has it today. Sure, I know I'm on the outside looking in and don't know how things really are done today, but it does make me wonder. I mean does making a weekly situation comedy really warrant a million dollars a show per character? Or even more? That boggles my mind, it really does.

Anyway, Mike worked incredibly hard on his new TV show, taping sometimes two shows a day for 8 months a year, and it ended up with his having a nervous breakdown, as mentioned before. It was a bad one. He survived it, but it was terrible.

CHAPTER 18

And then the wondrous Judy Garland came into my life. Oh how I did adore her. What a gigantic talent. Of course I'm always enthralled by people who could and can sing because my singing is so – well, let us say lacking! And Judy—no one before or since has had her voice. No one.

You know, when Judy Garland didn't win the Oscar for "A Star is Born," I was livid. Dumbstruck! All of America was just stunned! It was given to Grace Kelly for "The Country Girl." That stick! That expressionless stick of a woman. Beautiful, but with no range of emotions. Why did that happen? How could it have? Judy must have felt her heart breaking. It was horrible. A stupid, ugly mistake on the part of "the Academy." I'll never forgive them and many people won't.

I guess Kelly just won it because she came from great wealth and a very cultured background, and that always impresses the Hollywood people. Always. They aspired toward it, but of course never could rise to that level.

Garland was such an industry figure. She was important. She'd done so much for Hollywood from her childhood on, and her acting in that film along with James Mason and others was the best she'd ever done and certainly the best movie of that year or any other, as far as I was concerned. I didn't even know Judy then, but I hurt for her anyway. Still do, even though she's gone now. Everyone in Hollywood who mattered really was knocked at that terrible slight. "The Country Girl" was a boring, stupid movie. Bing Crosby was OK in it, but Kelly? All she did was stand around looking stricken. What a mistake. I know all of America was outraged at that.

I'll never forget the story of how Judy heard this news. She was in a hospital – not in the USA I don't think---and scaffolding and everything else was up against that hospital wall and her window to get her reaction to winning the Oscar. Everyone "knew" she'd get it. Her performance in "A Star is Born" was just simply stellar. Well, the news hit that Grace Kelly had won it and they tell me that scaffolding and everything else was instantly dismantled and removed and she was left there, probably as confused and hurt and upset as everyone else in the world. What a stupid, terrible slight to one of the world's greatest talents.

I met Judy when I was doing the play "Barefoot in the Park" in Boston. She was there with her last husband, and we all had to go somewhere to have our pictures taken. I still have that picture of me, my whole cast which included Margaret O'Brien.

Judy Garland. Guess what she did, this sweet dear woman! She hugged me when we were introduced, and we'd never met until then. Hugged me! All I'd really known of Judy was her work, and she knew mine and that's how she chose to greet me. It was just wonderful! We exchanged some words and I remember that moment so well. And I know the reason she hugged me was because I was sort of from her past even though we'd never met. We were from the Golden Years of Hollywood and we both knew we'd experienced a lot of the same things. (Of course in her case, she never even had a childhood because she'd begun so young in this business. Her voice as an adolescent was just astonishing. I did so love Judy Garland.)

Judy went on then to Europe and died soon after that in the bathroom of a hotel in London after taking an overdose of drugs. They found that she'd opened the window, but no one knows why. She was only 47 and had so very much more to give to the world---even more than she'd given already. She blessed our lives with her overwhelming talent, right from the time when she had the last name of Gumm and sang with her sisters as a little girl. Who will ever forget her luminous presence in "The Wizard of Oz?" Or how she looked and sang in "Meet Me In St. Louis." What a stupid waste it was to have her die so young and to leave us that way. I still grieve for her.

Before I close down this chapter, I'd like to tell you a little about my mother and her Hollywood experiences. She loved living there. Some of her friends and relatives would come out to visit her and she really didn't want to ever go back to St. Louis. I think she was dazzled by the endlessly good weather, and of course she didn't mind one bit being known as "the mother of Virginia Mayo!" She had a great time in that role, and she very much enjoyed meeting celebrities. My mother just loved walking down Hollywood Boulevard and in her later years we'd sometimes see her on the TV news strolling down the Boulevard, big as life and proud as a peacock!

But Mother was a practical woman, and she got herself a job at The Broadway, which was right near our apartment. It was a department store on Hollywood in Vine. She'd had experience in department stores, because she'd worked in one in St. Louis. She loved the work and could meet with a lot of ladies her own age, which delighted her. I don't know or care if anyone ever said "oh how horrible. Her daughter is that famous Virginia Mayo and that poor woman is slaving away in a department store when her wealthy daughter should be supporting her." Well, my mother always did whatever she wanted. She was feisty and stubborn and if she took it into her head to work in a department store while her "wealthy" daughter made famous movies, there would be no stopping her. I never asked my mother to go out to work. She did that on her own and loved doing it and she was a tough lady anyway, and if I'd tried to stop her, I would have been 100% unsuccessful. I wish people would understand the whole story before they pass judgment. If I'd had millions and millions of dollars and a hundred servants in a 50 room mansion, my mother would still have gone out to work in that department store!

I remember once she got herself locked into the store one night. She screamed and screamed "Get me out of here!" And someone finally did.

But inevitably, she had to go back to St. Louis. She'd gotten very old and various parts of her body were breaking down, and she had to go into a nursing home. My brother Lea and I made all the arrangements and it still hurts my heart to remember my dear mother crying, saying she wanted to come back to Hollywood very soon. She did not want to go back to St. Louis, but we knew it would be the best thing for her. Lea found her a Christian nursing home to live in and we both went to see her as often as we could. She died in St. Louis. She was 83 years old.

When she was dying, I was presented with a terrible conflict; I was in Canada doing the play "Move Over, Mrs. Markham." Doing that play wasn't always so easy. The British actors had very heavy accents and I had an awful time understanding them, but eventually I got the hang of what they were saying and could re-act to them properly on stage. The play was a big success and eventually went on to Canada.

Then came the hard decision. I was wondering whether I should I go home to prepare for my mother's death and funeral or should I go to be with my daughter Mary who was about to give birth to her first child, Lucas. It was a tormenting decision but finally I had to realize that I'd see my grandchild for the rest of my life, and I wasn't going to see my mother any more, so I went to St. Louis and did the play "Forty Carats" there and saw my mother for the last time.

CHAPTER 19

Let's talk here about George Raft. I appeared in a movie called "Red Light" with this so-called actor. Honestly, he was awful. He could not act his way out of a paper sack and I have no idea why he was ever even hired for any movie anywhere. (I've managed to block out everything about "Red Light," probably because I had to act opposite that non-actor.)

The man was an admitted friend to gangland folk, and a known gangster. In Havana he was a "greeter" for the mob at a gambling casino, and I have no idea how he ever got into films except for the fact that people thought he looked a lot like Rudolph Valentino. Years later in 1960 he'd again appear with me in "Jet Over the Atlantic." Castro was in power and Raft was unwelcome in Cuba. In "Jet" he played a director for the FBI of all things. But oh, what a lousy actor he was. He started in "cheap" films because a lot of actors did, to establish themselves. But eventually he was cast as a sheik and I suppose the studio hoped the public would accept him as the new Rudolph Valentino. I just don't know. But I doubt it would ever have happened. I know Mae West thought he was the cat's pajamas and they had a tumultuous affair, although it's hard for me to imagine that "actor" being tumultuous about anything. Oh, he was just terrible!

And after "Red Light" came one of my favorites, "White Heat," which I've discussed in a previous chapter. But it bears repeating—Jimmy Cagney remains, at least to my view, one of the most talented men the world has ever had. He could dance and sing and act in any role. Remember him in "The Man of a Thousand Faces?" There was nothing he couldn't do. Nothing! And he always took chances, too, instead of staying in one style of acting. What a guy!

"White Heat" was also directed by Raoul Walsh. Oh how I loved that man! And apparently he loved me back, because he gave me so many juicy, good parts and told me often how much he wanted to use me in his other films.

I would like to say here that while acting did come naturally to me, I got a lot of help along the way. Sam Goldwyn hired acting teachers for me, and I was given lessons sometimes with each film. (I was even given dancing lessons often. Jimmy Cagney who, not even knowing if I could dance, allegedly said "I want Ginny for that part," and he hired his teacher to teach me to dance the numbers in "West Point Story" in 1950.)

Even when I was not dancing in a film, I continued to take lessons on my own. I signed up with Nico Charisse's school. His wife was Cyd and that woman could dance like no other and I can't ever say enough about the beauty of her most gorgeous set of legs! She was in my classes too, and was a marvelous performer. I'll never forget Nico one day saying to me "I can get you into the movies, Virginia!" I had to laugh. What he didn't know was that I was already signed with Goldwyn for a ten year contract. But how sweet he was to have said that.

Florence Enright was a very well known acting coach, and she taught me a great deal. I know I was a good student. There really wasn't anything I didn't want to learn or couldn't learn and I objected to nothing. The studio people had a good student in me and I say this without any false modesty. I learned well and worked hard.

I'd go to Florence all the time before a film and she'd give me good advice and we'd rehearse a lot. She worked with me throughout "The Best Years of Our Lives" when I starred opposite Dana Andrews. I would want to have absolutely everything in place in my head before I faced any director! And I did! All the moves. All the words. All the "business" which means those things you do when you are or are not speaking, such as lighting a cigarette, scratching my head, picking things up and putting them down, doing normal things that would make an actor look normal, things that people just do in real life. Sometimes it's in the script. Sometimes it's spontaneous, off the cuff. For example, in that scene with Teresa Wright where I do all the talking and she just stares at me thinking "Oh, what a horrible woman this is" (because of course she's in love with my husband played by Dana Andrews) I had to have all the business done perfectly. I nailed it! I had to show the movie viewers how awful I was, and I got the point across. People gave Willie Wyler, that great director, a lot of credit for making me put on the performance I did in that wonderful film, and to this day, people think I won an Oscar for my role in that. They gave all the credit to Wyler, but you know, I had something to do with that good performance! That movie won nine Academy Awards. I didn't get one, but I remember seeing John Huston at a party once and he said "Virginia, you should get an Oscar for your work in that movie," but alas, I didn't get it. But I always still say that I got Willie Wyler his Oscar! After all, everyone said, after that movie came out "My God! If he can do that with Virginia Mayo......!"

You know, I really do want to say here that --- at least back then --- if you were pretty, and especially if you were pretty and blonde, you were automatically labeled "stupid." Not very bright. Makes me so angry! I've known an awful lot of very smart, very bright, very beautiful blonde women. And folks, I happen to be one of them.

CHAPTER 20

I'd like to go back to 1950 for a minute. I was thirty years old and had made a movie called "Backfire." This Warner Brothers movie had an awful lot of stars in it—Viveca Lindfors, and Gordon MacRae, Dane Clark, Edmond O'Brien. We had a really good director in that film named Vincent Sherman. I seemed to have been blessed by getting an awful lot of really good and really human directors. The good ones welcomed debate and discussion, differing points of view, and they'd quite often listen to actors, and would even make changes if what the actors said to them made sense. But generally I wasn't all that interested in arguing different methods and ideas and all. I just wanted to do my work.

But when I think back to 1950, it's the weirdest thing. I just can't remember anything about "Backfire." I've blocked it out for some reason. I just did the thing and can't remember one single moment of it! Can't remember the plot, never saw the picture and have disconnected everything about it. I guess it just wasn't important. But isn't that odd!

Mike and I were still living in his small house, but we'd had it enlarged and it was more livable. We called it "The Ranch" although it was only on about 1 acre of land. We had animals—of course my beloved dogs all the time, and Mike had horses. I wasn't keen on those big, smelly beasts as I've already mentioned, but he liked them.

But our dogs. Oh how I loved them and still love dogs. We had Springer Spaniels, I remember, liver and white. One was named Patrick. He got hit by a car in front of our home. Mike took him straight to the vet's and got him all fixed up, but our dear Patrick always had a limp after that.

And then we had Annie who was a sort of Irish Wolfhound-looking, although her parents were Doberman and something huge and shaggy. Our dogs lived in a corral with our horses.

I never lived in the so-called "Hollywood Splendor." Certainly we had maids to help with the housework because I wasn't there much since I was always working, and Mike didn't do housework. I drove myself to work and we never lived in a mansion. Not ever. We didn't live in the grandeur of a Gloria Swanson, for example. Of course Gloria had Joe Kennedy Sr. for a boyfriend. Now that's some story! But then it's been written about forever, so there's no point in going over it here.

But my point is that I was one of those working actresses who lived well, of course, but not extravagantly, not in the manner of a queen. After all, I made pittance--$100. a week with Goldwyn which gradually moved up to $1000. a week. When I left Goldwyn, that weekly salary obviously was gone for good, but since I soon began with Warner Brothers, they started me at $1000. a week. When my second contract was negotiated with Warner Brothers, I went up to $3500, with no options. ("Options," meaning they will pick you up and hire you for another year. But, the contract says that they can't just drop you, either.) So that was the most I'd ever made. People like Betty Grable and Clark Gable made $8000. a week, which of course was a fortune back then, and in general that was the yearly salary for many Americans. But my big salary and working years didn't last forever, and today I live on a pension from the Screen Actor's Guild (SAG) in the big house in Thousand Oaks that Mike and I built. Yes we have a swimming pool, but then so does everyone else in California. It's hot out here! And furthermore, it's no big deal any more. It's also not a huge pool, and it's definitely not for show. We use it, all of us, and have wonderful times swimming in the hot California sun.

My next movie was "The Flame and the Arrow" starring me, of course, and the incredible, sexy, stylized Burt Lancaster. Oh, he was just so handsome to look at. A former circus performer. Remember him in "The Killers"? That physique? That look on his face? A powerful man. A powerful actor. That was his first picture and was he ever impressive!

I enjoyed working with Burt. I use the word "powerful" a lot when describing Burt, but there really isn't a better word for him. He truly was terribly powerful, muscular, he moved like a panther, and it seemed like he was just high on power, and had to prove that all the time. That man could really steal a scene, (that is if I'd let him!) But then, no one can really steal a scene from a good actor, you know.

But those love scenes with Burt were extremely distressing to me. Terrible. He was just too rough. In the kissing scenes he'd grab my arms so hard he'd leave big bruises. Really! At night when I'd get undressed I'd find my arms covered with black bruises they'd have to cover with make-up the next day. And his kisses. Oh my! He would kiss so hard that once I thought he'd broken my front teeth! That's terrible! I had to run to a mirror to check them out. Who wants to lose one's teeth to another actor! Maybe he just didn't realize he was so muscular, but that just plain hurt. I look at that movie sometimes. I have the video, but there's really no need because it shows up on the American Movie Channel all the time, and I realize what a great film it was. The color is dazzling, the music spectacular and the whole thing is a marvelously entertaining film. Obviously a lot of people still think so, since it plays on TV so often.

Burt did all his own stunts, too. He had a fabulous persona and he made a fabulous impression. (To say nothing of possessing a fabulous body! I was happily married, but I wasn't blind after all!) "The Flame and The Arrow" was Burt's very own film and he wanted to make a huge impression. He did! He sure did.

Promotion of movies was a very big deal back then, just as it is now. Today, actors in films get themselves on every possible talk show to push their new films. Radio too. They'll talk about it anyplace they can. Well, we did that too, but only by appearances in big cities like New York, and on the radio, TV not being in too many people's homes in the 1940's and 1950's. And believe it or not, actors and actresses often went on tour to promote other films from the studio where they worked. It was done, and nothing was even thought about it.

And speaking of radio, I had a radio career too. Back in the forties and fifties, when a movie came out, one of the ways it was advertised was for a radio station to buy the script, rewrite it so it would "fit" a radio show and the actors would come and act out the movie for the listening audience. Whenever possible the actors from those films themselves would act the radio roles, but sometimes if a certain voice lent itself well to the plot and story, some other actor or actress would be hired for the radio show. I often acted on the radio in other people's films. And I did enjoy doing it, although acting for a camera and ultimately a viewing audience was more to my liking.

Remember that film I made with Bob Hope? "The Princess and the Pirate." Well, he and I acted the movie out on radio once, and I appeared sometimes on Bob's regular weekly radio show. It was always pretty tricky working with Bob. The man's insane of course, and he thought nothing of grabbing the pages of my script in the middle of the scene while we're standing in front of the mikes acting for a live audience, and ripping them up and eating them! I'm not kidding. There I'd be, standing with pages of my script missing and Bob's swallowing them. How on earth he did that without throwing up, I'll never know, but the man would go to any extreme for a gag and a laugh. I'll tell you something---one really has to dig way deep for one's acting training to pull one's self out of a mess like that. But I did it.

One of the ways was to be sure I knew the script almost by heart before the man pointed his finger at us telling us the show was to begin. Then as Bob chomped on my script pages, I could sort of muddle through.

Movies back then, as now, were sold everywhere in the entire world, but the studios couldn't make actors go to Europe to promote their films as I think they do today. Many actors wanted to go to Europe to do that, but of course during the war years, that was impossible anyway.

My movies are seen constantly on TV now. I think I could find at least one running, once a week if not more. People think I get a big check each time that happens, but no. I don't. I was paid for my performances and that was that. I know at my age I may not ever get any more lucrative parts so that I can make a lot more money, but I do get that pension whether I work or not, and it sure helps. Don't get the impression that I'm living in poverty. No, I'm not. I have to be careful however, but I do know I can live comfortably for the rest of my life.

During the time a movie was being made back when I was in films, even if we weren't going to be in any scenes for a month, we were not allowed to go on a trip or to be anywhere beyond fifty miles from the film. Things were very strict then. I wonder how that works today. I wonder if actors and actresses have the same rules we did. I somehow doubt it!

I'd like to tell you a little bit about Vivien Leigh. I know you're interested. Everyone is! I first met her at that Royal Command Performance in London I've already told you about. But here in the United States, I would bump into her on the Warner Brothers lot occasionally. I remember once she told me she'd just seen me in "West Point Story" and she just raved about it! I was so impressed that she would say those things to me, to take the time. She was lovely, sweet and just fantastically beautiful, and I feel sad that she ended up so badly. She gave the movie world so much. No one will ever forget her. What a presence. Remember her as Blanche Du Bois in "A Streetcar Named Desire?" Stunning performance.

Back in Hollywood in my day, films were usually made in the correct sequence—--in other words from beginning to end. I think today that films are made according to budgets. I once listened to a young actress on a TV talk show saying that she'd met her co-star early one afternoon and within an hour was naked in bed with him, playing a very steamy love scene. Well, I'll tell you, that would have been awful for me. I didn't have to know my co-star intimately, but I sure had to at least have gone beyond the hand-shaking stage. In any case, our movies never had such scenes anyway, thank Heaven. We were kind of able to get the point across without having to actually see people doing the deed. (And besides, movie sex was frowned upon and

82

always censored in those old days, so it wasn't an issue and so it just wasn't done.)

If, for example, a movie was about a woman who'd gotten pregnant without benefit of husband, it was done with a light touch and it was done with taste and often a lot of dignity. There was no need for long graphic discussions, descriptions or scenes of how she got pregnant in the first place.

It's my understand that in filming today, if an actor is getting a lot of money, they'll shoot his scenes first and kind of get rid of him, get him off the payroll! So I guess that accounts for the reason scenes are so often shot out of sequence. Location shooting has a lot to do with it too — seasons and everything. I don't know how the actors and actresses do it today, filming their final scenes first, their first scenes last and their middle scenes all over the place! How do they keep their concentration? Well, obviously they do. There are so many reasons why it's done that way today. I guess our way was easier.

I had a very big hang-up during my early acting career because I really did want to dance, but I'd really only been given dramatic, or sometimes comedic roles, none requiring dancing. Dancing, as you now know, was my first love. So there I was dancing in this wonderful black and white movie called "The West Point Story" with darling Jimmy Cagney, and also starring that indescribably beautiful dancer Gene Nelson, the funny big galoot Alan Hale, Gordon MacRae with his fabulously rich and mellow voice, and Doris Day. I didn't much like her because she was always agitating to get me off the movie which obviously didn't work. Doris absolutely did not want any women in her films, and if you watch them, you'll see there aren't too many! She wanted to be the only female star in her movies, I guess.

This next story does bear repeating because I'm very proud of the fact that Jimmy Cagney really wanted me to be in this movie, and so he had me work out and practice with his dance teacher and director, Johnny Boyle Jr. It was fun, a good film that still stands up.

And oh, can I ever remember those dance numbers. "The Kissing Rock," "The Military Polka," "The Flirtation Walk," the music and lyrics by Jules Styne and Sammy Cahn. Gene Nelson was with me in that film. Can I ever say enough about that good man and his talents? Probably not. But he was by far the best dancer who'd ever worked at Warner Brothers, bar none. Indisputably.

I'd very much like to state here that there was a point in my career when I had to really take a stand about my dancing movies vs. dramatic films. I loved doing both, but as I've already explained, dancing was my first love. I loved it then and I love it now. Anyway, I clearly recall that the studio wanted me to work in that Milton Berle film I told you about, "Always Leave Them Laughing." I agreed to do it, but gave them a caveat; if they promised to give me musicals to do, musical comedies too, I'd do the Berle film. I did it and the studio heads kept their word---they gave me six musical films. I am bringing this up again because one always hears about those big, bad studio people who are always so cruel and insensitive to actors and actresses. They weren't with me this time. They made me a promise, and they kept it and I'll never forget it. I was finally able to get back to doing what my heart wanted---to dance and sing.

Anyway, after films were ended, we usually had a big party and sometimes all us actors and actresses remained friends, but usually not. After all, believe it or not, show business is like any other. You do your work and you just go on home. Sometimes years would pass before I saw an actor or actress with whom I'd worked on a film, and it was always such fun to chat with them about the "old days," which maybe were only a year ago!

CHAPTER 21

The movie business was going along well for me. After I finished "The West Point Story" in 1950, I worked on "Along The Great Divide" with Kirk Douglas. He was awfully hard to work with. Walter Brennan was in that. He played my father, and my hair was short in that film. Women didn't wear their hair short very often in the days when this story was supposed to have taken place, so it was very interesting and kind of brave to do that! I couldn't have any elaborate hairdos anyway, long and flowing, because there was so much riding to do and it would have just gotten in the way. We went up to Lone Pine to make that movie. An awful lot of films have been made there. It's a lovely spot. Lone Pine has Mt. Whitney, the highest point in California, and it has the lowest point, Death Valley, so it's a treasure trove of great background scenery for movies. And I so loved being outdoors and working there. Lots of beautiful desert and mountain scenes, and the air was so sweet and pure. It was like being in heaven.

We went to England to film "Captain Horatio Hornblower" next, with Gregory Peck, and I want to tell you here and now, I've been kissed by a lot of famous men, movie stars, the most glamorous men in show business, but Gregory Peck was the best kisser in the business, bar none!

And what a nice man. Oh my. That voice. That face. That height. That class! Every actor wanted to be Gregory Peck. I really loved that guy. Remember him in "Gentleman's Agreement?" He played opposite Dorothy McGuire, my old friend, who has recently died. I will always miss her.

And then to see Gregory in "To Kill a Mockingbird," an enduringly marvelous film. Fabulous film. One of the finest in our entire industry. Oh he was (and is) just such a great actor, and a great man. So kind.

You know, the part I played opposite Gregory in "Captain Horatio Hornblower," like all the other "Lady So-and-So's" made me very uncomfortable. I always felt inadequate doing those "Lady" roles. Self-conscious. I always thought Greer Garson should have played them. She had that beautiful accent and spoke so well. I don't know why she wasn't cast in an awful lot of the parts I got. Oh, how I liked her. We became friends and I never stopped admiring her for an instant.

Speaking of feeling inadequate, I never really told anyone about these shaky feelings, but I can talk about them now, here in my book. I never argued with the studios when they offered me those "Lady" parts and thought "oh well, I'll just get it into my head and just do it and maybe I can say the words without sounding pompous." No one ever knew I was truly worried about being able to carry it off, and it was always challenging to me, but I just charged forward and did the job and I guess it was OK because people bought the tickets and watched my performance, and I don't recall ever getting any mail saying "You? As Lady So and So? Give it up, Virginia Mayo!"

I wouldn't ever seek out critiques about my work. If someone put a written criticism right in front of me, I'd read it, but I'd never ask people to run around and find printed (or even spoken) critiques of my work. However, if I did get to read them and they were negative, I'd always think "Oh boy, now they've caught me. Now they know I can't play those 'Lady' roles." And I'd squirm and worry—but only for a short while. I had work to do and couldn't waste my time dwelling on that sort of stuff. Living and reliving regrets is a stupid waste of time, if you ask me.

After that came "Painting the Clouds with Sunshine," I got to dance with Gene Nelson again. The plot was silly, and I wore shorts and a halter-top and was practically naked! In the picture, Dennis Morgan was in love with Lucille Norman. Now if you were Dennis Morgan and were looking at three ladies, Lucille Norman, Virginia Gibson, and me, who would you pick to love? It was a problem! But he picked me, lucky me! Virginia Gibson was a great dancer in the Muny Opera and was there three years after I was. She was red-haired, a darling girl and never really got the break she deserved, but her dancing was really wonderful to watch.

I guess one of my most famous dances was in "Painting." It was called "The Birth of the Blues" and I can say with no false modesty that it was one sexy number. Gene dances with me with one hand while he's holding and blowing his horn with the other. I did some pretty racy moves in that number and I'm very proud of it. It was great fun and an enormous effort on both our parts but we carried it off and it still holds up today. That was really something else!

Gene and I also did a dance entitled "Tip Toe Through the Tulips" and "Mambo Man." I truly loved making "Painting the Clouds with Sunshine" and wish it could be seen on TV as often as all my other films. I don't understand why it isn't, because it's among the best things I've ever done.

Dennis Morgan was a wonderful guy and I liked him a lot. He made the transition from musicals to drama very easily, but Warner Brothers did have him singing in a lot of films. So good looking. So popular. He was married to someone not in the business.

Did you know that the actor Tom Conway who was George Sanders' brother in real life? I acted with him, and of course I had a chance to act with George again in "King Richard and the Crusaders" later, in 1954. George eventually committed suicide because, as he said in his note, he was bored. Bored! He had such a fine mind, and oh, his marvelous voice. He had the world. What a stupid waste. I wish he hadn't done that, but of course there was maybe more to it than his just being bored. 1951 ended with my playing in "Starlift," a really nothing movie where they put a whole lot of stars in where they could perform their specialties. I did a little dance. That's all. It was terrible, and quite disappointing.

But in the main, if I may be immodest, I have to say I'm really proud of my films. Nearly all of them. I think they were wonderful and I never, ever get bored seeing them. I own an awful lot of them and am anxious always to buy more videos of my films, and as time passes, I hope to make my collection grow. We had such good lines to say all the time. We didn't have to curse and show people having sex. Do you think Cagney needed to use profanities to get his message across? No way! He could scare people without using those terrible words. Bogart and Cochran and all the great movie gangsters could make us fearful without uttering one single filthy word. We didn't have to do car chases and gigantic explosions and show people getting slaughtered in every possible horrible way. My movies were sheer entertainment. That's all. We just wanted people to see them, enjoy them and go home feeling maybe a little better about things. That was really our only goal. The shock system came much later. We didn't want to shock---we wanted to entertain and I know we did.

CHAPTER 22

Throughout all of this, all of the work in show business, and the glamour and thrills, something was missing from my life. I was searching in my soul for a spirituality, a religion I could embrace and practice. I began to think seriously about Catholicism and finally joined the Church and got confirmed. My newfound faith has given me much solace and comfort. I am glad I joined. Being a Catholic means a lot to me. An awful lot.

But I'd like to talk here about how I became very happily influenced to join the Catholic Church. It was when Mike and I were in New York City doing publicity for the studio when I first heard Bishop Fulton Sheen on the radio. I was in New York City helping to promote the movie "Giant," with Rock Hudson, Elizabeth Taylor and James Dean. (Back then we all promoted each other's movies.) Just as a little side bit here—during the screening of Giant, I was sitting next to a lovely young girl. We chatted and she said that she'd just gotten a script from Fox and that "I'll do the movie and that'll be the end of it." Her name was Joanne Woodward.

Anyway, Bishop Sheen had a weekly show—maybe it was even a daily show. I can't quite remember. Anyway, I was so taken by the things he said, so incredibly moved by his words and his voice (he was answering questions for me I'd all but buried,) that one day I said to Mike "Let's go and try to meet with this man Bishop Sheen." Mike agreed, so off we went to the Chancellery and asked permission to meet him. It wasn't difficult to meet him at all. Maybe my fame helped to open his doors a little more quickly than if I were not famous, but I know he was accessible to all people.

The Bishop was wonderful to us, so gentle. What a sweet, nice man he was. Just brilliant. He had a way of seeing things so incredibly clearly, and he could articulate things about faith and God, religion and spirituality I never could, and probably still cannot. I really do consider, of all the great and famous people I've met, that he was way up at the very top of my "favorite" list. How gentle. How intelligent he was. I miss him terribly.

Anyway, Bishop Sheen began to send me literature, books and records, not to brainwash me, but because I asked him for information about Catholicism. I yearned for something special in my life, a religion I could

88

agree with and follow, one that would give me joy and satisfaction. He gave me a lot of personal instruction too, as much as he could, considering that geographically we lived quite far apart. I haven't read all of his books, of which there are many, but if one does, one can easily learn what Catholicism is all about. His good words certainly struck a chord with me. I began to relax. I'd finally found the Church I'd been searching for all my life, either consciously or unconsciously I don't know, but I knew then that I had been on a long journey to Bishop Sheen's door. I became a Catholic.

The Bishop not only appeared on radio, but he was on television all the time too, and I wonder if he influenced more people than he ever even knew about. In any case, I am still, years later, years after that good man's death, involved with the Catholic Church. I have never looked back and have never once regretted my decision to take the instruction, get confirmed and to join. This Church has given me such peace and comfort. Do I attend mass every week? I do not. I no longer drive, and my daughter and her family attend another church, and so getting to Mass is difficult for me. But I keep it in my heart, so think that's OK with God, and with Bishop Sheen too, whom I know is watching over me.

Mike was Catholic, but a kind of watered-down version. He didn't go to church much. We sent our daughter Mary to Catholic school, but eventually took her out. She was a very sensitive child and that school made her extremely nervous. She was, in fact, a nervous wreck. They were just too strict. I hated to see my little girl so upset and scared every day when she came home, and every morning when she had to go to that school, so I'm glad we removed her. She was about eight years old and we put her in public school in Thousand Oaks, and it completely changed her outlook. She almost immediately became a very happy child.

We've always been asked if Mary wanted a life in show business, but she never once expressed a desire to do that. She just wasn't attracted to it and that was just fine with Mike and me.

But we both had to work if we wanted the so-called "good life," so Mike and I did many dinner theater shows like "George Washington Slept Here" (where Mike ad-libbed so much the audience howled with laughter, and he broke me up a lot, wrecking my timing, but I just simply loved it,) "Tunnel of Love," and the wonderful, funny "Fiorello!" where again Mike stole the show night after night by ad-libbing and cracking everyone up. He was so good on stage, and I don't think he ever really knew it.

But in spite of it all, in spite of all the separations from her parents as a child, Mary's become a happy and good mother. She is doing a wonderful job with Kent's and her sons, my darling grandsons Lucas, Evan and Dillon.

I never taught her to do that. She is just a natural at it, and learned it all on her own. I guess she learned a lot from Mike's and my being absent so much and decided that would never happen with her kids, and it hasn't. Mary breast fed her boys, but I never breast fed her because I had to go back to work almost immediately and was gone so much of the time, so it was impossible. But Mary grew up to be healthy and fine anyway, and I'm so very proud of her, every single day. I love Mary.

My work continued on through the forties, fifties and sixties on a very regular basis. The reason I was never threatened with termination on a movie set is because I didn't argue about a part, or about anything they asked me to do within that part. I just did what they asked.

Take Marlon Brando for instance. Oh boy. When he began on the stage, and yes, he's a brilliant actor, but anyway, back then, he'd make up his own lines as he'd go along, say whatever on stage he chose to. Well, OK, that's all well and good, but the other actors on stage with him would never know when to come in. Their cues were gone. It was a mess. Sheer chaos! Brando would look wonderful on stage with all his improvising, and the other actors would look stupid and blundering, because they'd be left stammering and stuttering, bumping into each other and not knowing when to say what. So unprofessional. Bad character. That was terrible to do. Just plain traitorous. All the other actors on stage with him would be left trying to pick up the thread of the play. It just wasn't fair.

Well, I don't know the guy so I probably shouldn't say any more. I never took any of those method-acting classes. That was strictly a New York thing, and it wasn't used in the movie industry during my day.

And I'll tell you one other thing; my motivation when acting wasn't method or Stanislavsky or anything else. It was the money. People who say money isn't everything are crazy. It is everything. Without it you can't own a car, can't get medical help, have a roof over your head, have clothes to wear or anything to eat, unless you spend your life going around to soup kitchens. You want to run around like a fool saying "the best things in life are free!! The moon and the stars are!!" then go ahead do it, but remember, you can't eat the moon and the stars, and you can't drive them or go to college on them or do anything on them. Money was and is very important to me. I worked hard, really very hard to earn mine. I had a family to support and it was money that motivated me absolutely. The fact that I happened to love being in show business was the icing on that cake!

And let's remember that being in show business can be a very chancy business. If your face is not seen for a while, you're forgotten. Gone. Into the vapors. We have to work hard and constantly to keep ourselves popular. (In other words, to keep ourselves working.) We can use publicists sure, but don't forget that agents and publicists have to take your some of money too. That's how they earn their money. It's a big circle and the only way to stay alive and healthy is to have money. If one handles money well, you can live comfortably and even give a lot of it away to worthy causes if that's what you like to do. Handled badly, you're living in the street.

Jack Warner, as I've told you, finally kept his word to me. He let me play in musicals, where I could dance. Dance! How happy I was. I never got his promise in writing, but back then, people in business, in my business at least, really did honor their words, (at least that was my impression) and they sure did this time. I didn't actually deal directly with Jack Warner on this issue. I dealt with one of his underlings, because it wouldn't have been right for me to approach the big guy. I didn't want to have any business dealings directly with him anyway. That's not how it was done. So I spoke with the people who worked with him about doing musicals again, and his was the final word. I could now dance! I was happy. Oh was I happy!

And so I made "She's Working Her Way Through College" in 1952, and it remains my all-time favorite movie. (I can't count the times I've watched it.) It was a remake, perhaps a little bit too soon, but still, of a film called "The Male Animal" in 1943. But they made it different enough to be successful and this time, it was with lots of music and dancing and it was in glorious color. My burlesque dancer name was "Hot Garters Gertie." Isn't that great? I got to wear fabulous costumes. Oh, how I loved, and still love, that movie. There is a dance scene in this where Gene Nelson dances (and does acrobatics) alone in a gymnasium, and it is a classic. I can't think of any other dance scene anywhere that can match this. He danced all over that gym, using all the gym equipment in his choreography---it is amazing and compelling to watch. You can't tear your eyes away. I think most, if not that entire dance scene was done in one take. The man swings from the rings, throws himself all over the horses and the parallel bars, flies across the mats, hangs and even sings while hanging from a rope, and when he does that, holding onto the rope in a sitting position, it's as if he isn't straining at all. And all the while he's tapping and twirling and dancing madly. Wildly! The music is fabulous. The whole thing is simply amazing—there really aren't words to describe it. If you ever get a chance to watch that movie, do it. I guarantee that even if you're not fond of dancing scenes, you'll love this one. What an athlete Gene Nelson was. His muscular coordination was astonishing. I don't think there was anything he couldn't do. Remember him singing and dancing in cowboy boots in "Oklahoma?" "Everythin's up to date in Kansas City, They've gone about as fur as they kin go!" He was just simply the best! What a dancer! And oh, what a sweet man. I loved working with him. If you get a chance to see that movie, you'll see Gene and me dancing on school desks and a piano to a tune called "I'll Still Be Loving You." Pretty tricky, but we never fell even once, not even in rehearsal. Guess it's fairly obvious that I loved Gene and we had a great time together. I was honored to work with him. He was one of those rare ones who also insisted in rehearsing and rehearsing. And rehearsing! Gene didn't tolerate mistakes. Nor did I, and I made sure I rarely made any.

Ronald Reagan was in that film too. He played a married man, a college professor, and did a credible job in that film. His wife was wonderfully played by Phyllis Thaxter.

There was another young dancer in that film too. She was new, and her name is Patrice Wymore. She played my rival, (her on-campus name was "Poison Ivy,") and oh, could this woman dance! She had the longest and most shapely legs I'd ever seen, and she was gorgeous too. Long reddish hair, fabulous eyes and skin. She was very tall, too. They put her in one dance scene wearing a pair of white and black sort of modified and very short bloomers and high heels. She was something to look at! The movie also starred Don de Fore.

Mr. Errol Flynn apparently thought Pat Wymore was something special too, because soon after that, they became married. (Actually Pat looked a lot like Nora Eddington who was Flynn's former wife. He preferred certain types, I guess.) They had a huge wedding with her whole family from Oklahoma in attendance. She was married to him when he died.

Errol was always in trouble. And the trouble nearly always involved females. There was that huge scandal when he was involved with a very young girl, fifteen I think. And he was always drinking and brawling, especially with John Barrymore and other actors, often Irish. How stupid. What a waste of time, money and humanity. What's with those guys anyway? Why do certain people think it's good to run around getting drunk, breaking up places and other people? It's so infantile and inappropriate. Honestly it gets me nuts when I hear about that sort of idiotic behavior. And the studios would always cover up things like that. Spencer Tracy was also a brutal drunk who would attack innocent bystanders in his drunken orgies, and sometimes really hurt them. People just walking by his table. It was terrible and crazy. The studios, by covering up all those asinine escapades and paying the damage bills, were really enablers. The guys who behaved like that never had to take any responsibility.

Errol could never grow up, and when he died in his fifties, his liver was a mess and so was his life. But Pat loved him and wanted him and got him, and I hope they were happy.

Errol Flynn was a real "movie star" in every sense of the word. He was a rogue, dashing, swashbuckling, so romantic looking. I guess in spite of his being so stupidly destructive, I liked him well enough. He was a man who had it all, but he finally destroyed himself. I guess he wanted it that way, or he wouldn't have let it happen. Maybe there was something bad inside of him that caused him to destroy himself.

You know, I really just don't get it. When did, and do, these people, these actors, find the time to drink all the time? To do drugs? There is so darned much work to be done on a movie, so I just don't see how they could and can do all that to themselves and still show up for work at 6 the next morning. I don't mean to sound naive, but what is that all about, anyway? What exactly does "being high" mean? I know I'll sound ingenuous here, but you know, if I have a good dinner and a great sleep, I get up in the morning and there it is! I have found my own so-called "high." And that's all I need to get "high." It's all so stupid and wasteful and for the life of me I'll never understand the drug culture. Life is all about work and accomplishing, and how can people do either one of those, if these dumb people are drunk all the time? And the cost! Not only to their bodies, but to their wallets. How do they support that stupidity? It's a mystery to me and I don't see the problem getting better as I get older.

Well, I don't mean to soapbox, but it's a big puzzlement for me. Anyway, Pat Wymore and I became friends even though in the movie we were sure enemies. She was going to perform in Las Vegas, I remember, and always was encouraging me to fly up there to be with her. She asked and asked me to go, but I always said no. I just didn't want to. Didn't feel like it. Wish I had, now as I look back. Today I regret that I did not go, but I remember being awfully tired a lot because of my work, and I had to sleep, and so I didn't go.

Pat still lives in Jamaica on a ranch Errol had owned. When her career began to close down after his death, she moved down there, since she'd inherited everything from him. A couple of years ago there was this huge party for all the people still living who'd appeared in musicals, and they flew Pat up for the occasion. I was invited and of course I went, and it was wonderful to see her again. I think thought, that the ranch just wears her out, and the sun has taken its toll on her. But she's still lovely and warm and nice and it was wonderful to see her again. We share a lot of memories.

In 1953 I made "She's Back on Broadway" which everyone insists was a sequel to "She's Working Her Way Through College" but it's really not. Steve Cochran was in that film, and I'd done five with him before that. He was a dear, trusted friend of mine. I will always love him and I miss him so much. Dear Steve.

CHAPTER 23

Our daughter Mary could not possibly have had a better father than Mike. He just simply adored her. Mike's life, I think, really began when he became a father. Mary Catherine was the apple of his eye always and always.

I still think about how he'd drive her off to Beverly Hills and there he'd buy her those beautiful and expensive dresses I've mentioned before, and have lunch at Nate and Al's. There would be so many movie stars there, and Mary would love it! She may be sort of blasé about meeting famous people today, but she had a wonderful time meeting them back then. Mary especially remembers meeting Judy Garland and remembers how kind Judy was to her.

Mickey Rooney is a good actor still today, but what a maniac! He's impossible to sit next to. He just simply, absolutely, never stops talking, and never stops talking about himself. And he takes endless credit for doing things he never has, such as giving Marilyn Monroe her name when she was still Norma Jeane Baker. Honestly! Don't forget that I'm good friends with Jim Dougherty, Norma Jeane's (AKA Marilyn Monroe's) first husband, and he was standing on a porch saying goodbye to his newly divorced (and so beloved wife) Norma Jeane when she told him about the name change. "Hey Jimmie," she said to him. "I've changed my name. Wanna know what it's gonna be from now on?" And she told him it would be Marilyn Monroe. He told her that was nice, she explained that the two names were taken from relatives, and they said goodbye forever. It was a sad day for Jim. But oh, what an exceptionally talented actor Mickey Rooney is. I'll give him that. I surely will! (James Mason even said that about him.)

In 1954, I made "King Richard and the Crusaders" with Rex Harrison and the wonderful George Sanders, (remember, I was in all that pain from Mary's birth, ouch!) and I'll talk about that some more here. (Following that in 1955 came "The Silver Chalice" with a newcomer named Paul Newman. I'll tell you about that film and Paul later.)

Rex Harrison was stunning in his role as Saladin, the lead Moslem in "King Richard and the Crusaders," and there was never anyone who could act as well or as interestingly as George Sanders. He had such a remarkable voice and accent. Rich. Beautiful. But he could be a little rude. No, pompous maybe is a better word. I guess Rex considered himself the finest actor around because he'd never hesitate to say to me, "Are you going to say the lines like that??" Pretty embarrassing, but eventually I'd just answer "Yes Rex, I am," and that would be that. Sanders played the King. Laurence Harvey had his first movie role in this film, and I played Lady Edith.

I'll never forget being in that film. Viewers may not have noticed that Lady Edith was in pain, but she, I, was, because, don't forget, I was still trying to recover from the Cesarean birth of our daughter Mary. I felt weak and my incision wasn't healing all that well. Normally at the end of every film I have a lot of pep left over, but not this time. I was exhausted, but will say here at the risk of sounding heroic, it really never occurred to me to not do the work. It had to be done. It was my job and I was committed and so I did it. But I also spent a lot of time sitting!

And speaking about having Mary, I'd like to back up here a little because I've just remembered a small and interesting story about the aforementioned Devil's Canyon, the movie in which I "starred with Mary." (You know, when I was pregnant with her.) It was made by Howard Hughes and was a really good picture. As a matter of fact, Howard "bought" me a couple of times in my career. Mostly I got along well with him and really had no special interest in that very strange man, but we did have an incident and I'll tell you about it here.

Howard was doing the inaugural flight of his plane -- I think it was called "The Constellation," and he'd invited all these celebrities to fly to New York and have a lot of on-board parties. I was included, and so of course, I went. We had ourselves a time!! It was incredibly luxurious and so much fun, and there was a whole lot of champagne flowing, so guess what I did? Yes. I did. I drank it and got sick. I mean SICK! I threw up, and that wonderful, darling, dear man, the ever so gallant Walter Pigeon got me an airsick bag and even held my poor head while I was vomiting. Ugh! That distinguished, classy man. I will never be able to forget what he did for me. He was so gentle and kind to me and tried so hard to ease my painful embarrassment. Oh, if his fans ever saw that scene. Can you think of anything more terrible? Well, at the moment, I can't. But just as he would have done it if it had been a movie, he handled it with all the kindness and grace a guy can handle a situation like that. I couldn't wait to land, and it was a long time before I drank champagne again! And whenever I had to see Walter again, well.........

When we got to New York, we all were assigned rooms (and there were more parties, and I even went to some. But no champagne for me!) I began asking the Hughes men when we could go back. I wanted to go back to California!

I then questioned the Hughes "authorities" even more, now demanding to know when we'd be making the flight home. You see, I wanted to get Mike, then still my fiancé, on the plane so he could go back with me. He'd just finished a play in New York City, "The Red Mill" with the famous Eddy Foy, and I thought it would be perfect if we could fly back on that marvelous airplane together.

Thus, being a complete pest, I kept asking and asking if Mike could fly back with us, and I just never got an answer. It was so annoying! They simply refused to answer me! They never said no. They just never said anything.

But now I know why. I surely do. It was because I was expected to play up to Howard Hughes. He had an enormous ego, Hughes did. Bigger than anything you can imagine.

Mike and I decided we weren't going to take this kind of snub from that jerk Howard Hughes, so we decided to go back to California on the train. We went across the country and had a lovely time and I'm delighted it happened like that because I'm left with a delicious memory of our trip together.

But oh boy, when I got back to the studio, I really got bawled out. I mean a lot. I mean loudly! I had to go and stand in front of some vice president, and he really laid me low. (I know it wasn't personal. The guy was just following orders and he had his job just the way I had mine. But still, it was embarrassing and it also angered me.) The reason for the scolding? Well you see, I'd insulted The King! King Hughes. And what Hughes wanted, Hughes got. That's it! They told me that he was a very big important man and that I'd committed a terrible faux pas by refusing to fly with him just because he wouldn't let Mike on board that plane. That I'd made a horrible mistake. That I may have caused the studio a great deal of damage which they'd have to fix, because I had had the gall to refuse His Highness. Oh, really. Come on now.

Well, let me tell you. It's a free country now, and it was a free country then, and just because Hughes flew me out didn't mean I had to go back with him, and furthermore, he certainly could have let Mike get on board too. It wasn't as if there wasn't enough room on that huge plane, I can tell you! Well, Mike and I took the train and that was that. I doubt Hughes even noticed or cared, but he got a real lesson in loyalty from me during that incident. Mike was to be my husband and where I went, he went. And vice versa.

But in spite of the fact that I got in so much trouble because of my stubbornness and what they perceived as my rudeness in shunning Mr. Great Big Deal Hughes, he still hired me to work for him in other RKO films. Well, maybe he thought he could win me. Where there's life there's hope, I guess, and he was not a man who gave up easily when it came to beautiful young movie stars. I was different, I suppose. I just didn't care to be "honored" by joining that man in bed. Or anywhere else, for that matter.

It's common knowledge that Hughes had ladies stashed all over Hollywood in apartments or hotel rooms and he'd go visit them whenever the mood hit and I suspect it hit a lot! Can you imagine that? He'd have countless ladies, sitting around (no TV then!) waiting for a visit from him. It was like a harem. Crazy! Can you imagine how boring that must have been? Nothing to do but sit in splendor and wait for His Majesty to arrive. If he would arrive! Those young ladies never knew. I hope they had a lot of books around. Or magazines, or knitting. Something!

Florence Enright, who was my acting coach, (and good friend) used to take care of his girls, by "teaching" them acting, to get them ready for the promised movies they'd (maybe) be in, all owned of course, by Howard. She told me about one night when she heard a knock on her door, opens it, and there's Howard Hughes. Florence invites him in, and he enters and begins to look all around the place.

Finally, confused, Florence cleared her throat and said "Uh--do you, I mean did you come here---uh, do you want to discuss your pupils or something?" Hughes didn't seem to want to discuss anything. He just seemed to want to nose around her apartment for some reason. Florence never knew why. How incredibly weird he was!

I'll never really know this, but I think to help feed his huge ego that Howard just wanted to know that ladies were waiting for him, stashed in apartments around Hollywood, so he'd be able to satisfy the kingly, harem-ish image he had of himself. And maybe he thought I (or some other actress) might be at Florence's apartment that night. I don't know for a fact that Howard was this way, but it's what I've deduced over the years. I could be wrong. He will always be a great mystery. Strange, strange man.

And in spite of all the publicity, it's my personal opinion that Hughes never even tried to seduce Jane Russell when she was so young and had been hired to do her famous early movie "The Outlaw" where it was hinted at, filmwise, that she got into bed with that cowboy. (Back in those days, movie people depended on people's active imaginations. They didn't have to

98

show every single living detail of a sexual liaison! Today---well, you know how it is today. I don't have to tell you.)

And another thing—remember that story about Howard's inventing this miraculous bra so that Jane's already ample breasts could be pushed up and out? Well, maybe he did invent the thing. I don't know about that, but Jane claims she never wore it, that she shoved it under the bed before that scene when Howard wasn't looking, that it was uncomfortable, it hurt, and besides, she really and truly didn't need it!

But Hughes did rule her life to a degree, put her on posters and all, and it did make Jane a big star. She had a good career because of Howard Hughes, but I don't know—I wonder if he ever went after her in "that" way. I don't think so. I guess Jane is the only one who knows the answer to that!

I love Jane a lot. She is one of those rare people who've become very famous but who hasn't forgotten her roots or her old friends. I hear she sees them often, friends who are not "in the business." Her mother was a preacher of all things! Jane is very religious and I see her often and like her so, so much. Remember those "Eighteen Hour Bra" commercials? Well, only Jane Russell could carry that off as well as she did, with no problem. Jane has never taken herself all that seriously. It's one of the things about her I find very endearing.

Jane began in show business early on. She actually was in a play in high school in Van Nuys with Jim Dougherty who, as I've told you before this, would marry Norma Jeane Baker who became Marilyn Monroe. It was a play called "Shirtsleeves" and Jane played Jim's mother.

And isn't it odd that they'd eventually end up in a movie together, Marilyn and Jane, called "Gentlemen Prefer Blondes." Marilyn I guess stole the show, but Jane was magnificent in that—tall and strong and very sexy, with a fabulous figure, all that thick black hair and oh, her beautiful, beautiful face. She and Marilyn got their feet and hands put into their sidewalk cement squares together at Grumman's Chinese.

Jane was a singer, too, and a good one. A tall woman, she once sang with a group of movie stars. Rhonda Fleming was in that group too. (That beautiful redhead, married to Ted Mann who at this moment is very ill.) They would sing spirituals. Jane Russell is just so great. It's obvious isn't it, that I like her!

CHAPTER 24

Nineteen fifty-four. Mary Catherine was now a part of our family, and I made only two movies in that year. I was thirty-four years old and really hitting my stride. It was around this time a very strange letter came to the Warner Brothers Studio; a fan letter from the Sultan of Morocco saying how much he adored and liked me, and also stating that "Virginia Mayo is tangible proof of the existence of God."

Well now. The press got hold of that and made much of it, (I think with a little help from the studio boys,) and I'll tell you here that while I don't normally pay much attention to stuff like that, this was unusual and pretty impressive if I do say so myself. I mean it isn't every day one gets a compliment like that, and from royalty yet!

After finishing "King Richard and the Crusaders" I went straight to work on "The Silver Chalice" with Paul Newman. (I mentioned before that I'd tell you about this film. Here goes.) Paul's character's name was Basil, and he was to be my love interest in the film. I remember being asked by the studio to work with him, to teach him what I could, and give him acting tips and all, and so I did---every day, and even on Sundays. I knew it was important for Paul. It was his first big break in films and this was a difficult role, and both of our roles really could be called "stylized." As a matter of fact, while I was working with Paul Newman, I was being coached by a great acting teacher named Elsa Schriber. She gave me very good advice on how to play my part. She was an excellent coach.

I will state here with no embarrassment that I wasn't deaf and blind to new actors and actresses on their way up. If I could help, I would. I myself got a lot of help along the way and had no problem sharing what I'd learned. And let's face it, working with a guy like Paul Newman wasn't exactly a hardship!

We all worked very hard on the "Chalice" movie and it paid off for me because I finally learned, with the help of Elsa Schriber, how to play that difficult part. Paul never liked the picture. He later got many more roles much more to his liking and eventually, as we all knew, drew an enormous following.

100

Paul Newman was extremely handsome, then and now, and actually was (and is) very gifted. But he'd never done any classical pictures, and this one was just simply too difficult for him. He was still a novice to the movie business, after all, and they probably shouldn't have expected this of him. (He probably should not have agreed to do the film, but he was young and eager to make a name for himself, as all of us were at the start.) Paul later showed how good and personable he was in subsequent pictures and he became one of our biggest stars. In fact it can be truthfully said that Paul Newman became a legend in his own time. I watch him every chance I get and he never disappoints.

Jack Palance also played in that film. He was an evil looking magician in the picture and that too was very stylized. He was quite good in his role.

In 1956 I made another film, called "Great Day in the Morning," with Robert Stack. Now that man has been around forever. I had seen him as a very young actor in early movies, and today of course, he does commercials and a lot of other things to keep his hand in the business, and he still has a long running TV show where the object is to track down people, both criminal and non-criminal.

He really impresses me, Stack does. He seems to hardly ever smile. I want to scream out at him, "Move your face, Robert! You look as if you're dead from the neck up!" But then who am I to tell him what to do—he's never stopped acting. And in spite of the fact that his face is a painting, I do like the man and we had a nice time making "Great Day in the Morning."

We filmed that movie in Silverton, Colorado. It was wonderful out there. I do love the outdoors, always have, and we got to do most of the movie outside. It was so high—10,000 feet, and just amazingly beautiful. I was so dazzled by the grandeur that I bought property there. (I had to be voted in by the city councilors. Those people weren't all that impressed by my fame.) But anyway, I was pleased to own that piece of land, and kept it for a while until I began to realize I'd never use it. It was just so high. Heck, the kids I'd see around that area looked all wizened and dried out, and I'm sure it was because they just weren't getting enough oxygen! And they had to weather all those storms! I'm sure Silverton has gotten built up now and modernized, but you know? It's never going to be anything but 10,000 feet high. Can't get any shorter. It's useless, at least to me. I found I couldn't stand to be up that high, so I sold the land.

Ruth Roman was in that movie "Great Day in the Morning" with me. I was asked which part I wanted, so I picked the role of the nice lady, the one who sold dresses. Ruth got the best part. I soon realized it was the better one, but I'd made my choice. And once I make a choice, I don't get everyone in a flap by changing my mind. Ruth was really a wonderful and compelling actress.

I'm not really actively trying to find acting jobs these days, but sometimes I think it might be nice to get a really juicy role again. Commercials? I'd do them, you know, like June Allyson and her Depends commercials, and Jane Powell and her Polident ads. But commercials are very hard to get. I hope someday someone will offer me a part in one of those, or at least let me try out for one. Well, I'll have to keep after my agent. I hope he's reading this!

"Congo Crossing." I was lent out to Universal to make that movie in 1956. It wasn't such a great production, but it was interesting. We were all supposed to be out in the Congo, of course, but this was actually filmed on a river in Los Angeles. (Same place they made that TV show called Fantasy Island with Ricardo Montalban, where that tiny French actor Herve Villechaize used to yell "De plane! De plane!" at the beginning. Remember?) In this movie, we'd travel along a waterway around a park. I guess it looked fairly authentic.

The script wasn't too bad, I guess. We were a bunch of people discarded by the human race in this jungle and on the river. (How many times have you seen that plot?!) In the film, I'm an outcast, down on my luck, I get on this horrid boat, big insects zoom around who sting us, and they were real! I don't know how they did that, but we had to have protection from them. ZZZZZZZ. Ugh! A black man gets killed and his friend grieves for him. Another black man plays the part of a doctor and I help him. All sorts of bad things happen on that dreadful trip!

But to my delight, Peter Lorre was in that film. Oh, he was a fabulous actor. He could be so humorous and so menacing, and he played that kind of back and forth role in many of his great films. Truly there wasn't anything that man couldn't do on screen, except of course, play a tall, dark and handsome leading man. Cary Grant or Robert Redford he was not! But Lorre was always a gentleman and a gentle man. Remember the big production he'd always go through lighting a cigarette on screen? He was very big on screen "business!" He'd hold the cigarette "European style," between his index finger and thumb, close to his chest, the burning end pointing out. What a character! I remember having some nice clothes in that movie and I did enjoy working with Michael Pate again, and George Nader.

But just before "Congo Crossing" I appeared in ""The Proud Ones" with that darling man, John the Baptist. No, really Robert Ryan, another actor who could play any role. He was tall and so handsome. What a face.

102

He played cowboys and businessmen and ancient Romans, evil guys, crazy guys, sweet husbands, military men and of course poor John the Baptist before his head was lopped off. Robert could play anything. He was up to all challenges and was a classic actor and he had a great career.

Jeffrey Hunter was a fine actor too, but he died too young, poor man. (Remember his role of Jesus Christ?) He had the most compelling blue eyes I've ever seen. Well, along with Paul Newman's!

The first movie I made in 1957 was "The Tall Stranger" with Joel McRea. I know I've already written about him, but it bears repeating; this guy was just as he appeared on the screen; decent, kindly, sweet and a real gentleman. I've been fortunate enough to have met some pretty terrific men during my career.

Unfortunately "The Tall Stranger" was not too good a film. I think the story wasn't strong enough and it just didn't seem to work for me.

I wasn't making any more musicals which saddened me. I loved doing them, but all the loan-outs now were for serious acting roles. Warner Brothers knew and understood that my greatest talent (and love) was for the musical comedies, but it wasn't to be any longer. I didn't know then that I'd be able to dance and sing on stage in another decade or so. I just knew in the fifties that I missed those parts. I still think a lot about that little Virginia Clara Jones kicking up her heels at the Muny, and later on in those great musical productions wearing fabulous costumes, practicing, loving it all. I miss her. I sometimes miss that young woman very much. And I often miss the little girl with the same name who learned all about show business from her Aunt Alice.

CHAPTER 25

There really was a lot going on in the 1950s, and in particular in 1954 when Senator Joe McCarthy began his famous hearings on "the Communist problem." I surely have strong opinions about that era, and especially about Communism. You may have already guessed that I'm a very loyal and patriotic American and I really had no time for Communists or Communism in my life or career. It appeared that they were out there, trying to influence many of us in show business to join up, carry the card, become one of them. Not I!

I suppose because I never showed any inclinations, I was never asked to join the Communist party back in the 1950s when it all suddenly became so popular. It was very obvious to anyone who knew me that I was for one-hundred-percent Americanism.

When the hearings were held and people "named names" it really didn't bother me one way or another. It was their problem, not mine. I really was in favor of all Communists in our business getting weeded out, and there were many known Communists in the studios. People would whisper to me that so-and-so is a "Commy." It became common knowledge, and I know I'd look at those who were suspect, and wonder how they could do that.

Communists did not stand for what America was all about and they were (and are) determined to bring our way of life down to their level. I was glad the problem was getting looked into and that the Communists amongst us were getting removed from the business.

I remember when that group of "lefties" from our business went marching on Washington DC and I thought that was awfully bad for them to do. It didn't hurt any of their careers, however, as I recall.

I think I must have known some of the directors and writers who went into hiding once it was discovered they had Communist leanings or were actually card-carrying members of the Communist party. The great director Dmytryk was one. He had to go to prison because of it. Years later I was on a cruise and Eddie and his wife were there too, and I found them to

104

be most compatible and pleasant. I liked them very much. I don't know for certain if Eddie named names or not, but I suspect he did.

Robert Taylor was very much a Republican and he definitely named names at the McCarthy hearings, and an awful lot of people in the business got very angry at him for doing that. But not I. Communist is subversion, and there's no other way to look at it. I am a staunch American and was glad when the government went after the Communists, and I was glad about those hearings. Why does anyone want to go to live in a Communist country when everything here is so perfect?

The movie "The Flame and the Arrow" in which I starred with Burt Lancaster was written by Waldo Salt, a very famous Communist writer. I know without a doubt that Waldo wrote a lot of lines in that movie which were outright Communist propaganda. He kind of covered it with a comedic flavor, but it was Communistic nonetheless. For example, he had me lamenting the fact that I was a Noblewoman and that I regretted that fact, that I was ashamed of being born into wealth. Now that's just plain silly. No one throughout history has ever regretted being a member of royalty, or being wealthy. Who would want to give that up to be dirt poor? He had me saying a lot of dialogue I didn't like too much, and it definitely was Communist anti-Americanism.

I guess Burt liked all that because he was one of those leaners. He definitely had given Communism some serious consideration. Now don't get me wrong. I loved working with Burt. He was a marvelous actor, so talented, strong, and handsome. His acrobatics were phenomenal. I'm not slamming him, but he really did sort of tilt toward Communism.

I know Joe McCarthy eventually went overboard a little. He'd become an alcoholic and really lost control because he began to call everyone a Communist, and I guess really caused a lot of innocent people to suffer and to lose their careers through the famous Blacklisting. McCarthy really had to be stopped eventually. He lost all credibility and died far too young from alcoholism.

CHAPTER 26

I'd like in this chapter to make a pitch for the return of the good movies of the so-called "Golden Years of Hollywood." I wish they'd come back to popularity. I'm no prude and can be as open-minded as they come, but oh, the films today are just so embarrassing for one thing. I have three grandsons I adore. (I know I've mentioned them before!) Lucas came first, then came Evan and finally Dillon, and I'd love to sit down and watch one of today's films with these three young men I love so, but I'm always nervous to do that because frankly it embarrasses me to be forced against my will to watch people having sex on screen, especially with my grandsons watching too. There's no way I'm not going to sound like a goody-goody, so I'll just have to say it—this is not good for children to see, or for me either, for that matter. I know kids today are very savvy about sex, but can't we just have two people falling in love in a movie and not displaying every one of their body parts in a passionate, rip-your-clothes-off, face chewing love scene? I'm not advocating going back to those silly days of showing married people in twin beds, but really, can't the camera cut away a bit more often?

And the movie violence. I know much has been written about this problem but with all the protestations about its being on screen and in video games, the violence continues. Years ago a big survey was put out trying to see if young children are affected by violence on TV and in the movies. Of course the answer was a resounding NO!, but I think that this might be because the survey was conducted by the film industry. But of course stupid, sick and pointless violence obviously has had a huge effect on young people. Today, kids kill people for little or no reason and the horrifying thing is that they have no remorse about it. If they end a young person's life because they want to own his or her sneakers for example, they just don't care that they have committed murder. Of course they know that in our country, punishment for taking an entire life away is only about 5 or 8 years, so what do they care? They get to go to a nice jail where they can get an education, have TV and workout rooms, and all the health care they could want. Why not spend some time there?

But I'm digressing. What I am hoping to see before I die is those wonderful old movies coming back. Surely they had violence in them.

Jimmy Cagney was always punching people out or shooting them in films, but there were no horrifying scenes of rape and car explosions and child abuse etc. My word, there wasn't even any blood in those old gangster films! Someone would get shot and you wouldn't see a drop of blood coming out of him—not even a hole where the bullet went in.

Oh I know what the chances are of getting those movies back again. Little to none. It's a shame. A terrible, hopeless shame. Back then, people could go home from the movies with good feelings and not troubled feelings. The films always ended happily and the singing and dancing in those great old films left people feeling happy, humming new tunes. It was entertainment. Today it seems we have begun to enjoy pain, misery and violence as entertainment. I am filled with regret over this. How did it happen? When did it get so bad? I wish I knew. I wish it would just go away.

All right, back to business. Sometimes during interviews people have asked me about the "loaning out" process, a very common occurrence in show business. I know I've mentioned to you as this book has been going along that I was "loaned" or "lent" to other studios. Here's how it works; if other studio people think you'd be right for a part, they negotiate with the people at your studio to "get" you. We actors and actresses never got any extra money for being loaned out, but I liked it to happen to me if it meant a good part. I enjoyed it a lot, actually and a lot of film stars did. I keep repeating this, but at the risk of sounding like an awful goody-goody, I really was interested in doing my work and getting paid for that work and not in making a big deal out of things like this. Work was work---I learned that in the Depression. Everyone should be grateful to have a job and to get paid for doing that job. I wanted to work in show business and I wanted to be paid as much as I could, just like any other working person in America. That was that. So when I got loaned out, I did my best.

It was still 1957, and I would make another film that year called "The Big Land" with my darling friend Alan Ladd. What a gentleman. What a gentle, sweet man. I'm still smarting about the way Hollywood treated that good soul.

Anyway, the brilliant actor Edmond O'Brien was in that film also. I played his sister, and it was filmed in Modesta near San Francisco. My memories of that film are very happy ones. Edmond was a wonderful man, a fabulous actor and I was privileged to know him. He's another of a large group of actors I miss a lot, and bit by bit, they're all leaving.

"The Story of Mankind" came up next in 1957. That was a terrible film. Loads of people were in it and no one had a good part. I played—are you ready for this? Cleopatra! (I wore a wig.) Oh my! I don't have much to say about this film, and truly I cannot remember the name of the producer. Honestly though, that man tried to force the most idiotic things on actors and actresses. He even once had Hedy Lamarr playing – get ready — Joan of Arc! I mean it was a joke! Silly. What a dumb group of people in The Story of Mankind. Groucho Marx was in it. Groucho Marx!! Please.

I finished all 3 of those movies in 1957, that last one, The Story of Mankind not being exactly one of my proudest moments. In 1958, I made only one film called "Fort Dobbs." I was back in the saddle again. (So to speak!) The actor opposite me in Fort Dobbs was Clint Walker. I had to support him. He was the star. Not I. He'd been in some TV show called, I think, "Cheyenne" for about five years and I think they thought he was good box office. I really had to do the best acting of my life to get through that awful film. He could be a nice guy, but was nothing much as an actor. Unfortunately he's been the butt of many a late-night talk show joke. His career never went on much after that, but it wasn't because of that movie. Although it may have helped!

"Westbound" came next, with Randolph Scott. I had an impacted tooth during that film and begged to get off filming for a week until I could heal, but I was told "no" by the director Bud Botticher, that I could not, that I had to play the part. I won't soon forget that man! He had given his girlfriend a part in that movie too. She played opposite me, and wasn't so good, but she was sleeping with the director, so I guess it didn't matter.

I knew Westbound would be my final film for Warner Brothers, and really my final film in America, forever. My ten year contract was up. I knew it. I knew it was over. And, even though he'd bawled me out a lot in the early years, Sam Goldwyn was very considerate of me that day, and did speak briefly with me saying that I would not be re-signed and that I was free to move on to another part of my career. He then turned and walked away. It was sad for me. I'd made a lot of pictures for him, after all. And while it was an amicable parting, it was still kind of awful for me to just drive away without a single good-bye from anyone. Ah, but truly I do try not to dwell on life's inevitable disappointments. I have to say now, however, all these years later, that this hurt me. A lot.

I then did a picture in Mexico City, an Independent Film, which means that the film is separated from the major studios with Guy Madison called "Jet Over The Atlantic." Guy was just great to work with, a truly nice man, and I enjoyed the experience because of him. He was my boyfriend in that film and really, he couldn't have been nicer. He made the experience a good one for me.

108

There were lots of other well-known artists in that film, such as George Raft, Ilona Massey, Anna Lee and George McCreedy. I recall that the studio was incredibly dirty. Awful. They really had to clean it all up before we could work there. It's odd the things you remember, isn't it?

While they were cleaning the studio, my stand-in and all the rest of us got to stay in a really nice hotel, the name of which escapes me, but we had a great time. Mary and Mike weren't with me then.

I got to do a lot of crying in that movie and even though I hadn't had a chance to see Guy much after our film together, I was greatly saddened to hear of his recent death.

CHAPTER 27

One day in 1961, my agent called and asked if I'd be interested in making a picture in Italy. Italy? No. That would be silly. I didn't speak Italian.

He explained to me that many actors and actresses were going to Europe these days to make films in various countries, and Italy in particular, and that all the actors would speak in their own tongues and it would all be dubbed later on.

"Do you mean," I asked him, "that I'd say my lines to someone who couldn't understand me, and I'd get lines said back to me I couldn't understand either?"

"That's about how it works, Virginia," he said. "It's going on all the time now. I think you should give it a try."

"Oh no!" I said. "I couldn't possibly do that." He mentioned the amount of money I'd be paid. "Oh yes!" I said. "I can possibly do that!" So Mary, Mike and I packed up and headed over to Italy for me to star in a film called "The Revolt of the Mercenaries." I would play a contessa, and there would be a lot of fighting. They seem to love to fight a lot in Italian movies.

I will admit that I really dreaded going over to Italy. I was very apprehensive about acting with a bunch of actors from other countries with none of us being able to understand each other, but as it turned out, it was a lovely experience, and a memory I still treasure.

Mike and Mary and I were put up in the very famous Grand Hotel in Rome, and it was everything I'd ever heard or read about it. Being in that grand Grand Hotel was just like being in an old movie! Wonderful! Beautiful! Rich! Sumptuous! We were treated like royalty.

And I got to see Pope John, jolly fat little John while I was in Rome, and what a thrill that was. I wasn't permitted to wear any make-up so I felt a little naked when I left the hotel, but as you know by now, I believe in playing by the rules. He was so kind to Mary and me when we went for our audience. She wore a white dress and veil, and I wore a black dress and veil. A car came for us and we were ushered into the Vatican. The Vatican! Little

110

Virginia Jones from St. Louis, Missouri! Wow! Oh, the fabulous works of art everywhere. We'd seen the Sistine Chapel while we were in Rome, but the artwork in the Vatican was just as stunning and fabulous. It was such an emotional experience for me, one that just can't be duplicated in any way whatsoever!

I began work on that film, and while it was extremely stressful to act against actors and actresses who could not understand me, nor I them, we all did have interpreters, and in time we developed a kind of rhythm and got the job done. The work was hard, but the pay was very good, and I really began to enjoy it.

When I wasn't working, Mary, Mike and I could sightsee around that glorious old ancient city of Rome and we loved it. We had a wonderful time together and saw so many fabulous things.

While we were there, we found, rather by accident, a lovely little woman, tiny, with small hands and a beautiful face, who consented to be Mary's nanny while we were in Italy. Mike and I were so relieved to have Audie (Adriana Onofrio) and in a short time, we found we just adored her. She was so good with Mary and they became very close friends. This was a relief to Mike and me. We could get out in the evenings now, if we wanted to meet with friends, and we'd know Mary would be well looked after.

When it was time to go home to America on a ship, we took Audie with us because Mary loved her so, but when we got back to the United States, we realized she just didn't fit in all that well and frankly, we just didn't have room for her in our home, which I guess we should have thought of before we brought her over. Besides, Mary would soon be going back to school, and what would Audie do all day? Thus, we made arrangements to send her home. Her family wanted her back too. They loved her, and didn't want her to be away from them that long. We put her on a plane for Chicago where some friends of ours met her, kept her with them for a few days and saw to it that she got to New York where she'd get on another plane or boat and get back to Italy. Audie was wonderful for our Mary, but sadly, she really couldn't stay with us forever.

While in Italy making the film, we were eventually told we'd have to go to Spain to do some final shoots, and so off we went and that was great fun, too, also still strong in my memory. Mike and Mary and I went sightseeing there, even spending some time in ancient Toledo, where they made (and maybe still make,) all those steel and metal things, such as razors, and back in ancient times, mighty swords. We took a tour through an old Spanish castle also and met the Count who was struggling to keep the old place going. It was undergoing major renovations. I often wonder what happened to that great old castle. I sure hope they didn't turn it into a parking lot! No, I suspect not. The Spanish are very proud of their country, and while Spain seemed to us to be a bit more primitive than Italy, it was still a simply amazing experience. But then, inevitably it was time to go back to work. We had to return to Italy so I could finish the film.

Quite suddenly we were told that there was no more money and that they would not complete the movie. I remember feeling angry and even sad about that, but I knew I'd get paid anyway, and so reluctantly returned to the United States, wishing I could have completed that movie. It was just against all my own personal beliefs to leave something so undone.

But then, amazingly, I saw "The Revolt of the Mercenaries" on television years later, so obviously that Italian film company found a way to complete it without use of my services or those of the other actors, too. So it goes in the nutty world of Show Business!

CHAPTER 28

One of my best and proudest memories is when I think about John Huston's telling me I should have gotten an Oscar for my role as Marie in "The Best Years of Our Lives," playing Dana Andrews' not so deep, not very sincere wife. And truthfully, I can say that I too really wish I'd gotten a supporting role Oscar for that film, but it was not to be. Well, the movie did win nine Oscars in 1946, so it hasn't exactly hurt my career!

I did win a number of awards as the years went by, during those Golden Years. I was "Miss This" and "Miss That" and those snippets of film, usually black and white, of my winning those awards, continue to show up on television, usually on those channels that have all the good old movies.

I can never forget the time I won something called "The Golden Boot" award, for my work in Westerns.

"The Golden Boot" -- I still keep it in the bookcase right near my chair,-- is an extremely heavy brass (although it does look like solid gold) rendering of a cowboy boot. It stands on its own small pedestal, and is about 8 inches tall and makes a great bookend. A small plaque is on it saying to whom it was given, (me!) and the date.

So I dress up and go to this big awards dinner to be awarded my Golden Boot, where a great many stars of Western movies were to be honored along with me, and I'm told that Dale Robertson will be introducing me. Well, to be truthful, he isn't my favorite human being, but that night he became distinctly unfavorite.

Out he comes. Now the deal is, when one introduces a movie star, one is supposed to talk about the movie star being introduced! But no, out Dale struts and begins to talk, and for about fifteen minutes, guess who he talks about? DALE ROBERTSON! He just went on and on, talking about being hired by Howard Hughes, and all the roles he's gotten and the great contributions he'd made to the American Western Movie. I thought he'd never shut up! I mean it was funny, I guess, but what a weirdo! And a rude weirdo, to boot! (No pun!) Well, eventually he got around to introducing me and I came out and got my big brass Golden Boot award. I should have dropped it on his foot. And now that I think back on it, I wish I had!

You know, Dale had a tiny bit part in my movie "The Girl from Jones Beach"---he didn't speak, but just stood next to me in a bathing suit with another guy, and then exited the scene. So in fact I was instrumental in getting him started, sort of, and years later he does this.

I guess I'm not terribly conscious about getting awards. I've won an awful lot of them. (Even once "Best Dressed," for my personal wardrobe.) I mean in show business, they're handed out like candy at Halloween and so one loses the thrill a little. I have so many in my home now, gathering dust, some sitting in sealed boxes, the occasions of their being given to me long forgotten. But even so, when I look at them, some do bring back a lot of very sweet memories, and sometimes I am sad that all those times are gone. I don't mean to suggest that I didn't appreciate these things being awarded to me. I did and do. It is such an American thing to do, isn't it? And as you know by now, I do love all things American!

CHAPTER 29

Mary was and still is a clone of her father Michael and when I look at her, I am sometimes startled at how much she resembles him. She will turn her head or speak in a certain way or make a certain gesture and it's like having my Mike back in my life for just a moment. Mary has strawberry blond hair, huge green eyes, lightly freckled pale, lovely skin. Like mine. I inherited my so-called "famous" skin from my mother, and I think Mary's got it too. I think she's beautiful. Neither tall nor short, Mary has and is a gentle soul. She loves animals and children and of course her husband, my son-in-law Kent. She is bright, a good friend to me and she is loyal and sweet to her many, many friends, and I know she is well loved.

One of the proofs I have of my knowing how much Mary is loved is that our home is always alive with comings and goings. There are people here all the time to see the some member of the Johnston family. The phone never stops ringing. Mary and Kent and the boys are very, very popular. In my day, we'd have said, "the joint is jumping!" It is. Absolutely always. I'll hear the door open and will look up from my reading, and a big, laughing bunch of kids will be roaring upstairs to one of the boys' rooms to play video games or watch TV or to talk, and oh, how they do talk!

But looking back, I realize it wasn't easy for Mary growing up with two famous parents. We tried to make her life as normal as we could, but it's never possible to keep a child's life ordinary or commonplace when the spotlight is always upon them. Many famous parents try, but it becomes very obvious to children at a young age that their folks are not just normal, average people who bake cookies, go to work and attend Scout meetings. The famous parents go to work too, but it's work that makes them well-known to millions of people, and this can be a burden to show-biz kids, no matter how hard the parents try to keep things low key and so-called "normal."

Mary had a hard time. It broke my heart when I had to leave her so often, but I had to go. I had obligations. I had to make money for my family.

But in spite of all that, I enjoyed motherhood. After Mary, as I've stated before, we didn't want any more children. As I mentioned before, I realized I was no breeder, and giving birth a lot wasn't something I yearned to do. Mary was all we needed in our lives, and we dearly loved having her.

I took her everywhere if I could, and remember taking her on the set sometimes when she was small. She would get very upset about the shooting going on in some of my films, and it didn't take me long to realize that to a small child, what they are seeing on a make-believe movie set can seem very, very real to them. And because children's minds are so literal, when Mary saw me being upset in my character's role, she would get upset too, and begin to cry. I had to explain to her that I was only acting for the movie and that it wasn't real, but she took it very seriously.

Mary never was an extra in a movie or anything as she grew up. Some movie people have their kids get small parts in their movies, but I never did, and besides, Mary never expressed the slightest desire to be in the movies. Frankly I don't think she has the talent for it and I don't care that she doesn't. I know that sounds as if I'm saying something negative about her, but I'm not. Just because people don't have talents in the world of acting does not at all mean they don't have great talents that lie elsewhere. Mary has many. She never had the slightest wish to be an actress, although I see in her sons a latent theatrical talent, and those boys sometimes think and even speak about getting into the business. (They say certain genetic gifts, such as creativity, skip a generation. I wonder.)

And so Mike and I never tried to force Mary, or encourage her to become an actress (or "actor" as they insist upon saying today, even about females in the business.) We just decided to let her go her own way, and she did.

Mary married very young—not even out of her teens then, but I didn't care. She married in 1972 at age eighteen, but I trusted her judgment enough to let her go ahead with her plans, and besides, Mike and I both liked Kent Johnston very much anyway.

Mary and Kent actually got married three times---they eloped and then had two "regular" ceremonies. (The first one was on June 6, 1972, the second in December of 1972, and the third a year later. Those two were very determined to spend their lives together and the marriage, now getting close to its thirtieth year, has been a remarkably healthy, happy and successful joining.

I flew in from Chicago for marriage #2 in Longmont, Colorado where Kent's family lived. (I've become very fond of his parents, Floyd and Dolores Johnston, over the years and every year go to spend some time with them at their home in that fabulous state of New Mexico.) They treat me

116

with such kindness and always leave me with the yearning dream to move there and have a ranch with lots of animals. Especially Llamas.

But anyway, that wedding was small and sweet and those two kids looked adorable. Mary wore her long beautiful hair straight down and onto her shoulders and had a veil draped across her head. She looked just so beautiful, and her Kent, so strong and young next to her---they were destined to be man and wife.

I wore cranberry and white—a cranberry turban with a cranberry and white dress---red on top, white on the bottom. Oddly enough, Kent's mother wore a cranberry outfit too, although we hadn't planned anything like that beforehand. Isn't it strange how those things will happen sometimes!

The third ceremony happened because I wanted Mary and Kent to be my sponsors for when I became a Catholic, and so they had to marry in the Catholic Church for that to happen. They are not Catholic today, as I am, but are very happy in their chosen faith, which is Lutheran. They attend church and they are very faithful attendees, as are their sons. Kent and Mary are doing a wonderful job with their children, my grandsons. I'm very, very proud of all of them.

Sometimes I am bewildered by all the happy commotion in the home I built with Mike that we all live in, but I love living amongst it all, and truly I always feel honored to be the mother, mother in law, and grandmother of this wonderful brood of mine.

CHAPTER 30

Before we moved to Thousand Oaks, Mike had begun to hint that he had something on his mind, something he wanted to do. He had a plan. Something was afoot!

And finally he told me; he wanted to go to Ireland. To Ireland! Forever! And so, as they say, it came to pass. Mike had been talking a lot about our going to live there. (He said he had family there. I wonder.)

My husband Michael O'Shea could sell iceboxes to Eskimos, and he'd begun a serious "campaign" to convince me to go.

What else could I do? I began to think about it, think about it seriously. Things weren't looking so good in America for me, career-wise, and Mike assured me that over there, the Irish weren't concerned with premiers and movies, that they loved the simple things in life, like family and home. He told me their values were right and good, maybe better than Americans' were. We wouldn't, he assured me, go to Northern Ireland where there was shooting and war. No, we'd stay far away from that.

I guess we were romantics---some might say foolish or stupid, because we never gave any thought to what we'd do for an income over there, and of course we were pretty casual about Mary and her schooling, just sort of assuming we'd find a suitable school and that we'd simply send her to it. I mean, there are schools everywhere, so we really didn't give that too much thought. We would get our child educated here or there. It didn't matter. It wasn't a problem. I wish we'd been more thoughtful about Mary's feelings however. I mean she must have been scared to think she had to attend a brand new school where she didn't know a single soul and to live in a foreign country also. But Mike and I, as I've said before, were romantics and always willing to just try something, and not give it as much thought or planning as we probably should have.

And too, I've always been a dreamer, and was never one to be bound to "the rules," as is evidenced, for example, by my going around the country in a car with two men doing an act with a make-believe horse named "Pansy." Everything else I've done in my life has had to do with not sticking to those crazy "rules" all the time. If I'd stuck to the rules, I'd be home in St.

Louis with twenty grandchildren and would be baking six dozen cookies a day for them. What a bore! No, taking chances and going my own way has been my rule! And going to Ireland without a whole lot of heavy, ponderous, boring plans seemed to be just exactly what we should do. Life for me has always been just fine, and each so-called "chance" I've taken has turned out to be a great experience. I expected our going off to Ireland would be the just one more of the same kind of thing. In retrospect, I know we should have given this more thought, but sometimes I guess you just have to jump when the opportunity presents itself. I guess I've always fancied myself an adventuress and was eager to explore new things, so in very short order, I eagerly agreed with Mike's dream.

We weren't particularly businesslike, and didn't plan much about what to do with our home, so we just left it, put it into the hands of some people we knew and trusted, and asked them to sell our furniture. This they eventually did. Kind of. (I think some of it went into their own home, to tell you the truth.)

Mike was responsible for taking care of all the animals we had on our "ranch" in Encino, as we liked to call it, and so they were gone, the horses and dogs, sent to places, to farms and homes. They weren't destroyed. (I hope. Mike would never have told me that anyway because I am such an animal lover.)

So there it was. I had no contractual agreements to honor and really nothing stood in our way. If we were to go to live in Ireland, then this was the time to do it. Everything was all set, all in place, so we just upped and did it!

We found ourselves on a plane headed toward Ireland, cutting all American ties. Our new adventure! We were excited. Thrilled! Mary? Well, she wasn't exactly thrilled, but she, poor child, didn't have much choice in the matter.

We began to live in Killarney in a wonderful hotel called the Hotel Europe. It was a German hotel, of all things, and was beautiful and extremely comfortable and nice. And, we discovered to our surprise, that a lot of Germans actually lived in Ireland. The two countries seemed, at least to me, to be friendly to Americans. I remember meeting a lovely young girl named Christina Decker, who worked at the hotel. She was German and spoke English, and we became good friends. I remember once saying to her, "Well, Christina, when you come to America, you can stay with us." And by golly, after we got back, she did. I got a letter from her saying she was coming, and wanted to see California and San Francisco. Uh oh!

Christina arrived about the time President John Fitzgerald Kennedy was assassinated and everything was shut down. But still, I took her to a studio and tried to entertain her. She didn't stay too long, maybe a couple of weeks, and then off she went to San Francisco. Really, she was a very nice person.

Mike and I decided to stay in that beautiful old Hotel Europe for a while until we got "the lay of the land." We put Mary into school immediately. Mary had never been exactly thrilled with this wanderlust plan of ours, and kept hinting broadly that she wanted to go back to America. Mary is very smart and she kind of kept this up for our entire time there. (I think it might be called something like the Chinese Water Torture! Drip drip, nudge nudge!)

Mike and I began to look at some places to buy, and did find one really great house, a two-story home. It only cost $10,000! Can you imagine any home anywhere today costing so little? We were delighted--—but something was holding us back. It wasn't the money—that was an inexpensive house for certain. We just didn't seem able to make up our minds. Something was keeping us from signing any papers, but what? We really liked Ireland. I mean it was no America, and we knew we'd have to make certain adjustments to Ireland's different standards of things, but we didn't mind any of that.

It was beautiful too, as beautiful as Mike had promised. A river ran through it that was glorious to see, the Limerick River I think it's called. The green there is like no other, and the people were all Mike said they'd be--- extremely friendly, helpful and nice, although I think, at least back then, that it was a pretty patriarchal society where the men ruled, or at least thought they did. I think some of the people there knew who I was, but they didn't seem to care or mind, and for sure they didn't seem to be terribly impressed, which actually was very nice for a change!

I remember one incident very clearly. Michael, Mary and I had been invited to a famous Irish author's home for dinner. We didn't know him very well, but thought that was a very friendly thing for him to do and so, eager to make new friends in Ireland, we agreed to go.

When we arrived at his home, this gentleman was extremely drunk. He was just a monster that night, horrible, obnoxious, and just getting drunker by the minute. His language was filthy, obscene! I can't even recall if we had dinner, but this guy was just quite simply smashed! Bombed! It was really awful. He became more and more loud and abusive, and his language was just disgusting, terrible, and right there in front of Mary, too.

120

Now I'm no prude and foul language doesn't make me faint, but I don't much like it or approve of it. I can handle it if I have to hear it, however.

As we stood there with that man spewing out his filth, Mike suddenly smiled and said that we had to leave, and he asked Mary and me to step out of the house for just a moment, to wait on the porch. When we got out there, Mike turned and grinned at us and went back into the house. I could hear sounds, a scuffle, the sound of a blow, a loud thud. Mike walked back out of the house, rubbing his knuckles, and again smiled, and said, "OK, let's go," and we got into the car we'd borrowed and drove back to the hotel. Apparently Mike had become so enraged at this famous man's filthy language around us, his wife and daughter, he went back in and "cleaned his clock" as they say. Mike decked him! Knocked him down. Maybe even out! My hero! My knight! No one was allowed to do anything wrong or bad in front of his family. The man, a famous playwright, was Brendan Behan. My Mike was great like that.

It was then we found out why it was we couldn't seem to make up our minds about staying in Ireland. One day, Mary came home from school, looked at her father and said, this time very forcefully, "Daddy, when are we going home? I don't like it here." Mike replied, as he had so often, "But honey, this is our home now," and Mary replied to him, as she had so often, "No. I want my other home. My real home." Clever girl!

We knew we'd have to maybe stop being so selfish and to think more about her wishes. She was our only child, after all, and if she wasn't happy in Ireland with us, then we should try to respect that, so we did. We changed our plans, decided to not spend the rest of our lives in Ireland and made plans to go back to California immediately. Thus, after just a few months on the Emerald Isle, we packed up our things, got back on a plane, and did just that.

CHAPTER 31

Our house in Encino was gone. I mean, it still stood there, but there was no way anyone could live in it now. What a horrible thing it was to come back to our home and see that it had been completely neglected, brutally vandalized. No one had been caring for it. We'd been promised, by that couple we knew and trusted, that the house would be looked after. Everything, and I mean everything was wrecked. We were devastated. It's not as if we'd loved that house, but it had been our home, after all, and our shelter, and I'd endured it. But now it was unlivable. It was truly awful. There is no excuse for this kind of thing. None.

Not only was our home gone to us, but many of my favorite and treasured items were missing, some of my clothing I'd wanted to leave there, to have sent over to Ireland for me, or to just save for me in case we returned. Expensive formal dresses, for example. It was pretty crushing. When I questioned the woman I'd left in charge of taking care of our things, she got kind of cagey and never really gave me a direct answer, so I don't honestly know what happened to those personal things and pieces of furniture and clothing I questioned her about.

Thus, we had to go to live in a motel. Neither Mike nor I had any money. Neither of us was working. We had hired a business manager, and had expected him to be investing our money all along, but I guess we should have been more careful and watched him more closely. Mike and I trusted people so blindly all the time. This so- called "business manager" apparently kept "investing" what little money we had, kept taking his "commission" for all the "work" he did, and we never saw any of our funds growing to any amount at all. As a matter of fact, our funds were shrinking, and rapidly. I don't know if this happens to all celebrities, but I suspect it happens to a lot. We're so busy doing our show business things, we don't pay enough attention to the people we hire who may be cheating us, and of course they count on that fact. As a group, we seem to be very naive and trusting.

We finally realized what was going on and fired that guy, and hired a new one who then did a respectable job with our funds, invested well and made money for us and in time, became a good friend. We knew from the

122

start we could trust him, but still, we did check up on him more often than we had that first guy. He'd been honest and helpful from the start, so you see, there are good folk out there who can in fact be trusted utterly. He has since died and I miss him very much. He was very good to and for us. He was the manager, and his name was Leonard Oliver.

Since getting back into our home was now impossible, and since we were forced to move into a terrible motel (which was very expensive and dreadfully uncomfortable for us,) we contacted some Realtors and they showed us a house which we sort of listlessly bought, not really being "in love" with it. But it was a port in a storm so we moved in and stayed there. I just simply disliked that house however. It never felt like home, so since I wasn't working, I began to take long drives during the day to look for another home for my small family and me.

I well remember that wonderful day. I was alone in our car driving north on Rt. 101, just looking at the scenery, hoping to find another home and I suddenly came to a wonderful place called "Thousand Oaks." I'd read about this area. It was named thusly because the area had many, many Oak trees, certainly more than a thousand, but nonetheless, it was named Thousand Oaks. The air was good and clear, quite different from the San Fernando Valley and as I gazed about me, I had a sense that it was a magical area, free and open and pure. I was so taken with this area, and its rural beauty just took my breath away. I'd always loved the great outdoors and there was an awful lot of it around there! I kept driving around and around, looking at it, smelling the clean air, loving the serene beauty. It didn't take me very long to realize that this was where I wanted to live.

I found a development! Its name was Starlight Ranchos. Starlight Ranchos! I kept saying that pretty name over and over to myself. I immediately found a Realtor and was shown a model home and instantly liked that, too. It was a lovely home, the kind of place where, when you walk through the door, you sigh. You're home.

I drove straight back to that other (awful) house where we were living, and told Mike about what I'd found, and the very next day we went out to look at the wonderful, clear and beautiful Thousand Oaks area. Mike fell in love with it too, as quickly as I had. I knew he would. We both agreed it was the perfect place to spend the rest of our lives and to raise our daughter. Somehow, we scraped up enough money and bought a lot.

The very next day, we began to have our new home built. It was happening very fast, but that was fine. Things have a way of happening fast when everything fits, when it is "supposed to be." The price of a new home for us was so inexpensive we would have been very foolish to not snap it up.

We were thrilled that the cost was something we thought we could afford, and we could. Our new home would much resemble the model we'd seen, although we wanted the beamed living room ceiling higher than the one in the model home. That, we were informed, was "doable" and it was done.

This house would be large, sprawling, beautiful, with a strong Spanish influence, the architectural style in California since California was discovered! It still is. Today one can still see much Spanish influence in the architecture of California.

The windows in our new home would be large and tall so we could see the beauty around us. Our huge front door would open into a large foyer. To the left would be a long sweeping staircase which would to lead to the 3 large bedrooms and two bathrooms upstairs. To the right of the foyer would be our big living room, somewhat formal but inviting and comfortable. At one end we'd have an enormous fireplace, and to the left of that would be our ample dining room, (which we'd be able to enter through the living room and the kitchen,) perfect for putting in a big table to entertain our family and friends, which, in the future we did, often. Straight ahead through the foyer, would be a really big eat-in kitchen, where we could put, at the left, a large table, even a big comfortable couch! Off to the left of our eat-in area would be a substantial maid's room with its own private full bath, and a full laundry room. In time we'd change the attached garage into a huge playroom because my grandsons were growing into great hulking young men who absolutely always had friends over. So that room would be for a pool table and those crazy computer/TV games, whatever they're called, and big couches. My family today has weekly gatherings of many friends who come over to watch, of all things, those dreadful wrestling shows. They eat and laugh and have a wonderful time together and when I hear that din, I again realize the joy of having, and living in this family.

To the right or our large kitchen/dining table would be our kitchen, big and roomy with white ceramic Spanish tiles on the countertops. Our kitchen windows would overlook our patio and swimming pool, not an enormous kidney shaped thing so popular in Hollywood at the time, but a nice size, perfect for Mary and her friends, (and us and our friends too,) and just beautiful to look at in the sunlight with its sparkling aqua colors, and flowers all around it.

Upstairs, Mike and I would have an enormous master bedroom with a full bath at one end, and one wall of all closets. We'd have a lot of storage in the upstairs hallway, and we'd have carpenters put in shelves and cabinets. There would be another large bedroom in the hallway and a third at the end and a bathroom off of that. Mike even had a small room all for himself off the hallway where he could put his own TV and other treasures and he could "hide" there and have privacy.

We loved planning our home, Mike and I, and when it was done, finally, we were very, very happy with it. I live there still and it remains my favorite place in all the world. Thousand Oaks of course like everywhere else, has grown a lot, and now there's a fairly steady stream of traffic outside my living room windows, but still it's pretty quiet, it's clean, wide open and safe, and I do enjoy living here.

I remember one day when Mike came home lugging a gigantic set of mounted longhorns. They were just so beautiful! We hung them above the thick slab of wood which served as our wall-to-wall mantelpiece, right over the center of our fireplace, and they've been there ever since, and look simply fabulous. We don't have anything much more along that mantelpiece, and so the view of those horns is spectacular!

Mike and Mary and I moved into the house in Thousand Oaks in the winter of 1965, and I've never left it.

CHAPTER 32

My husband Michael O'Shea had always had a great sense of duty, of patriotism, much more than other Americans I think, and I wish everyone today had his fervor when it came to all things American. I admired that in Mike and I admire it in anyone and hope people see the same characteristic in me, because it is in me. Strongly.

As I've already mentioned, he had a great love of police work, but when he'd tried to join up years before in New York City, he'd been told he was too short to be a cop. He'd never been in a war and I think he would have gone had he the opportunity or chance. No, I know he would have. He so wanted to go, to fight for his beloved America. He loved his country passionately and always wanted to give something back to it, since he felt strongly he'd been given so much. And finally, finally, he thought he found the chance to do that very thing, to give back to the USA.

I have to say at the outset that what Mike was planning disturbed me greatly. I remember crying when he told me the plan, and begging him to not do it. Pleading with him. Reminding him that he was a father and that Mary loved him. I remember Mike's saying gently to me that yes, he could be in danger, and it could all even result in his death, but that he had to do it. He had to. It was his chance to be a hero for the United States even though no one would ever really know. And finally, I realized there would be no convincing him, that he would not and really could not turn this down. I stopped begging him.

I'll never forget those days. It was 1963. At first Mr. George Bland of the FBI asked Mike to become friendly with the famous criminal Mickey Cohen, which Mike thought about and eventually did. He knew that Cohen liked a certain barbershop called Rosthchild's, so Mike would go in there for a haircut and would make an opportunity to chat with Cohen just as if he were a "regular guy." Mike could talk with anyone about anything, and had no trouble getting Mickey Cohen to spill all! And, since Cohen was very fastidious, he was at the barbershop a lot having his hair cut just so and having his nails done. Therefore, Mike pretty much knew where he could find him. My Mike had so much courage.

Mike, now full of information on certain illegalities Cohen willingly gave up, would then tell the FBI all he had learned about the gangster.

Mary remembers how Mike would go to FBI man George Bland's home so he, Mike, could tell George all of what he'd learned from Mickey. She says she can remember playing with the Bland kids while Mike and George sat at the dining room table talking quietly, a nearby radio blasting loud music (she remembers Glen Miller!) so no one could hear their conversation. What did the FBI want Mike to tell them about Mickey? Truly I have no idea.

Because of Mike's success with Mickey Cohen, and because he had such a strong memory and could remember everything so well, (he was especially gifted at recalling the most minute details of his conversations with Cohen,) the FBI then approached him again in 1964 and asked him to spy on the patrons at the Friar's Club in Hollywood. The Friar's Club is a place where showbusiness people—back then it was all men and I'm not sure if it still is that way or not—gather for food, drinking and card playing. You know, "guy stuff." But anyway, the FBI wanted Mike to listen to all the gossip there and to remember everything he saw and heard. In particular, they wanted Mike to find a man called "Doc Stature," and report on him. I don't know what the FBI wanted him for and I'm not even sure Mike knew, but it just didn't matter to him. If the Federal Bureau of Investigation thought Michael O'Shea was important and smart and could help them, he was their man. He was finally "fighting for America."

Now Mike was not a member of that club originally, so the FBI paid the dues for him to join up and belong. It was very expensive to be a member of that exalted club. The Friar's Club is an actor's club, where rich men can have lunch and can spend time there gambling. What was very difficult for Mike, after he'd joined and had become more or less of a fixture, was when all the members kept twitting him about showing up so much, so often. They'd say "Hey Mike! What are you doing here all the time? Why do you come here every day? You don't drink, you don't gamble. You don't even chase women!" Mike was enough of an actor that he could laugh and make a joke and kind of get past that. Sometimes he'd even say, "Oh, don't you guys get it? I'm a spy!!" and they'd all laugh. Mike could sometimes take foolish chances!

Apparently the FBI was convinced that many members of the club were involved in criminal action. They asked Mike to go there every single day to spy, and learn all he could. Considering that Mike didn't really love to act that much and wasn't into pushing his career, he told them he thought he could "fit that into his schedule," so against my desperate, tear-filled pleadings to not become involved, Mike went ahead and got involved anyway. He agreed.

And plead I did. I was not acting when I wept, and begged him to not get involved. I was afraid. I was frightened that something terrible would happen to Mike, to me, to Mary. It was a bad thing, and I knew it. But Mike would not listen to me. He wanted to do it. He was a cop at heart and this fit perfectly with what he really wanted to do in his life, for how he perceived himself. For Mike, all of this was like a dream come true.

I am still not sure what criminal activity they'd asked Mike to find, although over the years since his death I've had a lot of time to piece things together and I still think and think about those days. Members of the FBI do keep their secrets, you know. What I'm sure of is that they were after some big men in certain businesses, and they were interested in illegal gambling.

Mike was proud that he was able to find out that someone had drilled tiny holes in the ceilings above the people gambling in the Friar's Club, enabling him to see the cards. Somehow, and I've never learned how, the man looking through the ceiling holes would get word of what the cards were to other members at the table so that they could win lots and lots of money. The scheme apparently worked very well. I've never quite understood how those holes were not noticed, but I guess the guys who did the drilling knew more about how to make the holes inconspicuous than I could! When my Mike found out about the holes and the subsequent scam, he was able to report it to the FBI.

I am not even sure if Mike knew everything the FBI wanted or why they did. Sometimes I think he just blindly did what he was told and either didn't ask any questions, or didn't want to, or was afraid. In any case, he never told me what was going on, and that may be because he was afraid for me to know. Afraid Mary or I would get hurt. Afraid we'd slip and let something out that would endanger us. I'll never have these answers.

The FBI put a phone in Mike's room for him, and so every night when he got home from the Friar's club, he got on the phone to tell them everything he knew. Well, not exactly "them." Mike had one contact, one man with whom he spoke.

I remember after we moved into our beautiful new home in Thousand Oaks, there were guards around sometimes. And once they knocked on the door, and told us with real concern in their voices that we had to go away, to go to Ojai, to a funny little hotel up there. To hurry. We left immediately. If the FBI warns you that you may be in trouble and that you ought to flee, you flee and you don't ask questions.

Do I know why they asked us to go away? This time, yes. It was because some hit man had come into town and they were afraid that he'd come after us. Mike put fancy iron grillwork bars in front of all our big, beautiful windows and they are still there today.

The FBI did pay Mike a little bit of money, a very little bit, for doing this work for them, but he'd have done it anyway, for free. Mike so loved America he truly felt this was a chance for him to do something noble and good for his country, and I think those guys really played that up to get him to join them. I guess today it would be called "pushing his buttons." Well, it worked, and what a terrible thing it was indeed. And what a terrible price I know my husband had to pay.

What people don't get, I think, is that the crooks rule things like gambling and all the other horrible stuff in our country, and honestly I don't think we're going to ever beat them at their game. They are just too good at it. As soon as we crack down on one part of criminal activity, it all just pops up someplace else. It's a pretty bad thing and as I grow older I feel more and more helpless about it all.

The FBI people promised in the beginning of all this that Mike, when they began to make arrests, would never have to testify. Testify about what? Mike never actually told me and I was never sure, but I have my thoughts on it. They promised him they would fix it, and oh how they lied to my darling husband, my dear naive husband Mike. In his fervor to be patriotic and helpful, he utterly believed them. But why not? Those guys can be very convincing, and anyone not in that business would have believed them. It wasn't as if Mike was stupid or anything. He just trusted them, and when later on he had to in fact testify, he felt so terribly betrayed. He had to get up in front of those dangerous men and be pointed out as "the fink." He couldn't believe it. It all just broke Mike, just completely broke him. Everyone turned against him. All his so-called Hollywood friends. Mike could hardly get any more work. It was a horrible thing. Terrible, and I shall never forgive what they did to my husband.

When Mike went to the FBI offices later on asking if there were any reports or records on his activities with them, they very dramatically tore up all the papers with his name on them, right there in front of him just to "prove" he'd be safe, that he'd never be implicated. (Furthermore, they were not anxious to have the public know that they'd enlisted a "civilian" to do their dirty work.) Do I believe they were telling him the truth when they tore up those papers? That because the papers were torn up his name was safe? I don't know that for certain, but no, I personally don't think so. I think it was a stupid but successful trick they probably do all the time to convince innocent civilians who help them that their names would never be brought up. Do I think they had many copies of those records elsewhere? I don't know that either, for a fact, but I'd probably bet my life on the fact that they did. Do I think someone could today look all that up about Mike under the auspices of the Freedom of Information Act? I don't know. Maybe. All I can do is have faith that those papers they tore up in front of him were all the records they had. I guess I sound a little gullible. I guess I sound a lot gullible. That tearing up of the papers routine was probably well-rehearsed and men were trained to do it. Probably was done all the time to convince honest, law-abiding, innocent "helpers" that their personal records were clean.

All of this lasted about three years, with the trial being held in 1968. It was hell. Mike was called terrible names. He'd been so brave to go into the Friar's Club in the first place, thinking he'd get to clean up a mess in America, and now everyone was turning against him. I remember going to the club myself one day, and the main gangster of Los Angeles was there, John Roselli, right there staring hard at me! I stared straight back at him. What gall. What a creep. Mike had discovered that Roselli had not been born in Chicago, as he always stated he'd been, but in Italy, making his welcome in America a little dicey. Roselli ended up being a stool pigeon, and later on I'm glad to say he was killed by "family members" and put into a barrel (they had to cut his legs off first because he was too big for it) and was dumped in Biscayne Bay. Horrible. Like a bad gangster movie! But he deserved it. Those guys are completely cold-blooded, even to their own.

But eventually Mike got a TV series called "It's a Great Life" with Jimmy Dunne and Bill Bishop that ran for 3 years, and it was very funny. People loved it. It was hard on Mike, and after all he'd been through, he had that nervous breakdown I spoke of before, and after a while the show went off the air, as they all do. I think that show is even still run occasionally. But nothing special happened for him after that, career-wise. I've sometimes asked myself if Mike would do it all over again, knowing what he knew, and I have always known the answer. It would be yes. He would. Mike wanted to help the country. Maybe he did. But in the end, the country – at least the FBI – didn't help him back.

130

CHAPTER 33

When I was in Houston, Texas, to do "Follies," (where I at least tried to do the show but never could get the routines "down pat" because a young woman who was taking care of Maxine Andrews would never relinquish the room----well, keep reading. That story comes a little later,) I finally just stopped agonizing about not getting enough rehearsal time, and went to visit with my two good friends Marge Crumbaker and Betty Mitchell. These women were never in show business. We'd struck up an acquaintance while I was doing dinner theater in Texas some time before that.

These are two women I greatly admire, and we became good friends and have remained so for many years. They are wonderful, brilliant ladies. Very creative. Marge Crumbaker used to write a column for the Houston Post newspaper and quit that job, "to just live!" (I even took my dear grandson Evan to see them once when I went to visit them.)

These women both "do their own thing" as people say today, and for that I admire them. I guess it could be said I was a woman who did her own thing too! Anyway, one of them, Marge, is building a house for herself and Betty to live in on the Gulf down in Texas. Betty is so accomplished and builds homes for millionaires, so I can't wait to see the new one she's building in which she and Marge will live. Those two women are so beautiful and bright. Marge just finished designing and building a home for a woman who writes romance novels, so I guess there is an awful lot of money to be made writing those things! (I can truly say I've never read one, but someone out there sure is reading them. Frankly I think it's just dumb stuff, but who am I to criticize?)

Betty Mitchell has been living in a high-rise in Texas, but she and Marge have had possession of a hotel in New Branfels, and it's a wonderful place, old fashioned, over a hundred years old, they'd redecorated it, and I stayed there. It was fabulous, so much fun. But they sold it because that's what they do. I'll drive with Marge and she'll point out buildings and say "Oh, I own that." They buy, fix up and sell buildings, and they always make the places better. I admire anyone who makes our wonderful country look beautiful in any way at all!

When I took Evan to Texas to meet Betty and Marge, they took us to a huge old ranch where we got to know the owner. She was so old and had long, grey braids. This woman drove us around her ranch in her antique truck, and I was thrilled to see that she raised Long Horn cattle. I hadn't known they were still around. Remember how I'd told you how Mike bought about that huge set of long horns to put above our mantelpiece in our Thousand Oaks home? While I've never ever seen a pair larger than those, it was wonderful to be amongst the real thing that day. I'll never forget it. That woman would feed that herd, call them by name--- "Here Gussy! Here Mable!" As an animal lover, this just thrilled me.

Betty and Marge tell me all the time that they'd love for me to move to Texas and be with them, but I'll never go there. Texas is terribly hot and I've heard the cockroaches are enormous! I know it's a beautiful state, and I think I could happily live near my two good friends. But, my real dream, my "geography dream" as I've said before, is to move to New Mexico and have a small ranch there, big enough of course for some animals, and for dogs. Always room for dogs because they are my dearest love. (Mike and I had horses and dogs all over the place when we had the home before the Thousand Oaks home.) And I'd have a Llama, too, if I moved to New Mexico, maybe a couple of them. They make wonderful pets I hear, and they do protect all your small animals. Predators won't go near sheep or cattle if a good strong Llama is on the scene. It's been proven over and over. I've even seen films of them in action. What a lovely beast a Llama is. Those eyelashes! Oh I do love them.

I'd want to build an adobe house on my ranch. Do you know that they are waterproof and soundproof? Bug proof? Everything good is in an adobe house. I'd love to do that. I would. I've looked at homes out there and they were wonderful. The air seems to be so pure too, but then I live near Los Angeles where the air is mostly soup, so any air would seem clearer. But it is better and fresher in New Mexico. I don't know if I'll ever get there, but dreams, they say, are good to have, and moving to New Mexico and having a ranch is one of mine.

Anyway, my family have their lives very well set here in California. They're happy here, so I know they'd never go with me. But you know, sometimes I think that the planning is the fun of it all, when it comes to having dreams. We may never get our dreams to come true, but planning for them is so good to do, and good for a person, and good for the heart and soul. It kind of keeps us in mind of goals, and as we all know, quite often the goal, when achieved, isn't nearly as much fun as working toward it was.

132

I guess I've been around long enough to know that life often gets in the way of our dreams. But on the other hand, I've seen an awful lot of my dreams come true, so I can say clearly and without hesitation that I am happy.

CHAPTER 34

I'm asked often if I'd like to work again, and I find that I'm of two minds about this. I could not really dance any longer, although because of my dancing years, I know I move well now. (I once tripped over one of our dogs on the stairs and fell to the bottom, but because of the dance training I had, I knew how to fall and really did no more than bruise myself.)

Dancing as you now know, was my very first love. I have a good life now with my beloved family, and our two adored dogs Carly and Topper, a Jack Russell. We used to have Spanky who was Carly's son, but he's died. They were rare Border Terriers, and I miss Spanky a lot. I frequently see friends, often from "the old days." I'm in touch by phone with a number of people. But sometimes the yearning comes back to me. I'm told my voice is still clear and "listenable," and so I think if I were offered speaking parts, such as commercials or readings, I could do it and I'd enjoy it. No, I'd love it! (And I still have a feeling that because of Mike's difficulties with the FBI and those unscrupulous people I am perhaps on a "don't touch" list. I will just never know.)

I do still have an agent but he really isn't working hard for my cause, if in fact I do still have a cause. Maybe he doesn't think he should work hard for me because I'm not the beautiful young thing I was once. Who is, when they age? I refuse to be one of those awful movie stars who look like mannequins, so thickly made up, desperately trying to keep their youth. I've always been a "what you see is what you get" person, and while I've never objected to enhancing my looks for the camera or the stage, I refuse to look like a painted old clown. My skin, they tell me, is still beautiful and once again, I give my mother credit for that. Her skin was like mine—pure and like satin. Pearly, they tell me. I was blessed to get that.

It's hard, I guess, for those of us who have been in, and then out of show business for a lot of years, to not want to get back into it. Even though I can't dance up a storm any longer, I can still get around just fine and I know I can act. It's sad, it's sad that those of us who worked so hard in the industry are just overlooked now. I mean after all, not all parts in films today are for the young, the dewy and the skinny. And while I could never cuss and talk dirty the way actors and actresses do in movies today, I am sure there must be parts where that isn't necessary. Honestly folks, I am not being a martyr, and I do love my life now, but sometimes when I see myself in those old films, sometimes I do yearn a little, ache a little to get back into it. It was a glorious time, that, and I miss it.

Now I quickly want to state I'm no Norma Desmond. I don't sit around in a darkened room and watch my films waiting for Cecil B. De Mille to call and then say, "Ready when YOU are, Miss Mayo." How absurd! But I do watch my old films. I have videos of many of them, and it's fun to see them again, and to remember how it all was. And it was all so very good.

Happily, I am always amazed to see that I'm still getting a lot of fan mail, and what is very interesting is that I'm getting it from younger people too, people I'd think would have no interest in my old films. They send me money for a picture, and often send me self-addressed stamped envelopes, too, which I very much appreciate because postage can be very expensive, especially for those large envelopes, since I usually send out a signed 8 x 10 glossy.

I remember the fan mail I got at the height of my so-called popularity. Getting that letter from the Sultan of Morocco was great fun, although I never actually saw it—the studio people told me about it. I recall too how the poor people working for the studios told me that I had to handle some of the fan letters myself because it was becoming too much for them. Now I don't think that the big stars of today have to deal with their own fan mail, (and I've read about how their actually reading it is discouraged because any kind of friendly greeting could invite a stalker) but back then, I did have to take some of the burden off the fan letter people and hire other people to deal with it. It's a huge chore, enormous. But one I welcome. After all, it's the fans who've made us famous, who've paid to see our shows. We in show business owe the fans absolutely everything.

It was time to move on, after that last film Westbound had been made. I drove away and went home to Mike and Mary and wondered what I would do with my life next. Money was a problem, as ever, and it had to be earned.

It was then I began work on that film I told you about called "The Revolt of the Mercenaries," filmed in Rome. We, Mike and Mary and I, were there for six months, and everything was paid for. It was a great vacation!

I would not be out of work long. I did not know it, but the stage play period of my life was about to begin. Within a few months of my leaving the film world, I got a call from some play people in Las Vegas to do a play for them. I liked that offer. The play money was very good then. I don't know if it is today, but back then it was a very lucrative way for an actor or actress to make a good living.

I realized that show business for me was getting into the dumps, so it was good for me to move on. Working for a live audience had a certain appeal for me. I was going to get a pension from the studio, but we really needed more money, and it was up to me to supply it, as much as I could.

CHAPTER 35

The problem of money was growing again. We always needed it and never seemed to have enough. Mike, Mary and I had returned from Spain and I knew we had to have more money in order to live decently. My film career was truly over now, and I'd accepted this fact and wasn't lamenting it. I've always been able to accept the things life has handed me without whining.

But, I had to make other plans, and it was my agent who came through for me. He suggested I go on the play circuit—to do live performances. On stage! This would be really different for me, but I was eager to begin. I know it would mean I'd have to be away from home a great deal, but the money would be very good. And besides, I really still wanted to perform. Was it a burning need in me? Perhaps. I think I'd worked too hard to just drop the whole acting thing. I did want to work again. It was a matter of necessity. And, it was a matter of my love of acting, too.

Thus, I began to start this brand new phase of my life. And I can say looking back, I really enjoyed it very much. Now don't forget—this wasn't exactly brand new to me. I'd already been on the "live" stage, back in the days of The Muny Opera, "Pansy the Horse" and when I worked with "Old Banjo Eyes." But since then, it had been all film making, and I was eager to get back out there and perform for a live audience. There's something so satisfying about working in front of living people; one gets instant feedback. In the movies, one has to wait months and months to get a reaction to the entire movie, and scenes have to be played over and over from all different angles, etc. to no reaction at all, save for the crew watching the whole thing, and they're really not encouraged to applaud or react in any way at all. But, in a play, poof! You do it and it's done, and if you don't get it right, well then you're in trouble! It's a whole new thing, new timing, new experiences. I knew I'd love it! I just couldn't wait to get started.

My first time out on the live stage was to be in Las Vegas. I never would have thought this possible, but my agent got the deal made, and I went for it! It made me a little nervous to have to fly up to Vegas to talk with the producer about the play he was producing because I was just sure he'd be a gangster! But in spite of my fears, I flew up to the Thunderbird Hotel with my agent and this thug looks me over and says, "Take your hat off." I did. Then he said, "Well, she's OK. She'll do." I mean the guy didn't even ask me to audition, or read for him, or anything. Well, perhaps he'd seen my movies or something, and liked me from those. Who knows with those guys?

Anyway, I got the role and it required a little dancing which pleased me a lot. Unfortunately, this play was produced by a young guy who didn't know a single thing about producing. Or directing! But guess what? The gangster guy did! We rehearsed a lot, for a really long time, so we could open in July. This young producer, the man I didn't like, (what a phony!) was married to Gunilla Hutton, and he was putting on the show for her. (She had really big bosoms!) They had a child together, and she of course had a part in the play. She had a lot of songs to sing (I didn't have any because I'm not a great singer) and was an original play, actually a musical (my favorite, as you know.) It was called "That Certain Girl," and honestly, with all of my misgivings and all the very hard work, it turned out to be a very good show. Really remarkably good! It was about a Jewish boy who falls in love with a Christian girl, and the young lovers talk on the phone all the time. I played the girl's mother, and Mickey Callan played the boy. He was just darling. He danced and sang and was just so very good! The cast was also truly good. My husband in the show was the famous Dennis O'Keefe, and the father of the Jewish boy was played by the wonderful Walter Slezak. I was surrounded by the best, and when you're surrounded by the best, you DO your best. I did. We opened with a full orchestra and the stage had 2 sides, Christian and Jewish!! The show lasted six months and got very good reviews, and it was a full house every single performance. I had a ball! Las Vegas may be huge and glitzy, but I had a wonderful time doing that show and it was a very big hit, I'm proud to say. And a great way for me to again "get my feet wet" on the stage.

Then they decided to make the show run longer and so to save money, they cut songs out, or worse, they cut them in half. They cut out a lot of the orchestra, too, and reduced the dance numbers. One of mine was completely cut out. That crazy producer/director said to "Cut that dance number! Cut that other dance number!" Mine! One was a Spanish dance but as it turned out, I was really very glad about its being cut, because I just couldn't do that twice a night. It was terribly strenuous.

The show just kept going on and on. The reviews were good. But that Gunilla made so much trouble for everyone. She'd see me in a new dress and go whining to her husband so she could get one too. And she'd get it! She was pretty and so was a big hit in that play. Finally it just had to end. It kind

138

of dwindled down. Dennis had to leave and so he did. He went back to California and died. I wish he hadn't died. He was just excellent in that play and such a nice man. The guy they got to replace him was awful. A no-name.

They then started screwing with my billing. Now I can stand for a lot of things, but NO ONE screws with my billing. They placed my name under the title. That may not sound like such a big deal, but to actors and actresses it IS a big deal. We work very hard for our livings, and the proper placement of billing is very, very important to us. I know people not in show business might find that to be childish or arrogant. It isn't. When someone in any profession works hard for recognition and it's taken away from them, it's indeed a very big deal. I've worked much too hard for that. So I called my agent who was with the William Morris Agency, and complained. He was one tough agent and he got those guys on the phone and they quickly understood that they'd better stop fooling around with my billing. They stopped and fixed it immediately.

But then, just to make us more miserable, the powers that be decided to hold back our checks! The man who took Slezak's part was a TV actor, (I wish I could remember his name) and they held his check back along with the rest of ours. So he and I went to see the big bosses. We were simply outraged that we weren't getting paid! We told them off, demanded to know why this was happening, advising them that we wouldn't put the show on one more time unless we got paid properly, honestly and immediately! It took them a while, and they finally paid all of us, but you know, we shouldn't have had to do that. We shouldn't have had to go and demand what was rightfully ours. After all, we'd done the work and because of our good performances, the play was very popular. The bosses had decided to not do their parts in this. It was difficult for me to make that scene and to confront them, but I did it with the actor from TV, and we won.

And then, "That Certain Girl" was over. I began work on "Move Over, Mrs. Markham," and got the news that my mother was dying. She'd been happy back in the nursing home in St. Louis where Lea and I had to so reluctantly put her, even though she told me so often in letters and over the phone that she'd really loved living in Hollywood with me. But as things turned out, coincidentally, my agent had gotten me the show to do right outside of St. Louis after I'd finished "Mrs. Markham." I'd be able to work and be near my mother at this sad time.

But, it was one of those difficult situations for me, because Mary was having her first baby just then (it was 1974 and Lucas wanted to be born back in California,) my mother was dying, I had the show to do, and I just didn't know to which place I should go. Mary needed me, but I knew I'd never see my mother again if I didn't go to her. I knew I'd see a lot of my new grandchild, so the choice finally, after much wrenching thought, seemed clear. I went to St. Louis to say goodbye to my beloved mother, went back to Vancouver to work on the show, got the news that she'd died and went back to St. Louis to her funeral.

People do ask me sometimes if I ever had to audition for these plays. Well, we were the stars. And one was always billed as the star, so that was just simply out of the question. Anyone who wanted me to work for them understood where I'd come from and had seen my work, so for me to audition would have been ridiculous and demeaning. I'd appeared in so many plays, often being the only remaining cast member when the play moved from city to city. I'd acted in countless films. My credentials were such, I reasoned, that I did not have to do auditions. And if I were asked to, well, you can be sure that I'd shoot a look at the asker that would just about wither him!

Another question actresses and actors are often asked; "have you ever forgotten your lines?" To this one, I can answer YES! It hasn't happened a lot, but the memory of that's happening has been burned into my brain forever. What a horrible, terrible feeling that is. Imagine, standing on a stage with all those eyes on you, and you "go up" on your lines and just cannot make them come to you. Not good! Sometimes the other actors on the stage can help you out,---that is if there ARE any other actors on the stage at that moment. Sometimes the line will come back to you. Sometimes you just stand there and babble out something, anything to get through that moment. And some actors, I've heard, actually turn to the audience and explain the situation.

Now I understand that audiences really do enjoy that sort of thing occasionally. It humanizes the actors and makes the audience feel as if they're a part of the whole thing, that they're "friends" with the actor, and they can "help" him by laughing good-heartedly at the situation. It's never gotten to that point with me, thank heavens, but when I've forgotten lines, well, I'll tell you, your entire insides just simply turn to solid burning ice and there's little you can do but stand there in terror! I wouldn't wish it on my worst enemy.

And about audiences. I don't know if there have ever been any studies on the psyche of a collective audience, but as a group, they can be the strangest of people. Sometimes my cast and I would give the absolutely finest performances of our entire careers, and the audience would just sit on their hands and not even react. Other times, we'd be sloppy and silly, doing

140

a very poor job, and the audience would clap and shout and give us standing ovations. There is absolutely no figuring audiences out! Go figure, as people like to say! Go figure.

Ah, but none of us in this business, if we're smart, ever forget the importance of the audience and the fans. Never. Without them, there would be no us.

Did I love to learn lines? Never. It was my most unfavorite part of acting. I used to LOATHE doing that. I remember when I'd be making movies and I'd come home just wiped out from working all day, and I couldn't play with Mary or talk with Mike too much because I had to lock myself away and learn lines. I guess I had a pretty good memory though, because I managed to get them into my head and get them straight when it was my turn to speak them!

I did so much love acting in that fabulous British comedy called "Move Over, Mrs. Markham." This was performed in St. Petersburg Florida although we broke it in in Vancouver at a nightclub called "The Cave." Oh, it was such an extremely funny show. Satire. Farce. A really big hit! We rehearsed with English people and I had a hard time understanding those thick, mumbled British accents. It all just sounded like a bunch of sounds to me! But I finally began to be able to understand them, and to get the timing right and we got the play up and running. Americans love and loved it (I am sure that play still goes on somewhere,) and it was extremely popular when I performed in it. Not because of my role in it, but because it is so well written and so agelessly funny! Completely adaptable to Americans.

I traveled around to many, many locations with this play and again found myself as the "anchor," the one cast member who stayed throughout it all to the end. Some of the newer actors weren't funny and that would annoy me greatly because this play, when done right, had laughter coming from the audience almost every minute! It was a comedy, and having actors in it who couldn't handle comedy was a sin. It would get me so angry, but I'd work with them and hope for the best.

I used to work in that play with a man named Art Kassul, a truly funny actor who used to work a lot with Betty Grable when she was doing plays.

And then came the wonderful, irresistible "Barefoot in the Park." It really doesn't get much better than that, was written by that most splendid of playwrights, Mr. Neil Simon. (I did get to meet that great writer one time, and that's something I'll always remember. Pure genius.)

I played the role of the mother, and had those terribly funny scenes where I nearly collapse after having to climb all those stairs to get to the young couple's apartment. Margaret O'Brien played my daughter until she had to leave the show, and then Patty McCormack took over. You'll best remember her as the blonde pigtailed child in crinolines and plaid dresses who kept on murdering everyone who annoyed her in the movie "The Bad Seed." When Patty left "Barefoot," the part went to Gigi Perreau. Lyle Talbot also appeared in this play, and what a fine actor he was. Oh, I've been so blessed to be able to work with these great thespians.

My dear friend Jack Mullaney was in this play too. Jack and I became very very close, and I miss him dreadfully. He's dead now. He literally drank himself to death. A very troubled man, he could never come to terms with his sexuality. I personally think it's a crime that our society today still condemns people for being born certain ways. I find gay people to be the most interesting and creative around, always fun and funny, making an awful lot of straight people boring by comparison. Gay people, like all people everywhere, have contributed so much to the world, and in particular to our business. I'd never criticize gay people for being gay. That would be the same thing as criticizing someone for having brown eyes, as far as I'm concerned. No one has that right. My poor, dear friend Jack Mullaney having to die that way because he was forced to keep this deep dark secret. It's a shame and a crime, and it's stupid and wrong.

Anyway, we traveled all over the country with this remarkable play, "Barefoot in the Park," and it lasted well over a year. I had a wonderful time performing in it. I never got bored even once, doing that play. I never minded that I had sometimes an entire new cast to work with when we moved to another theater in another city. I could adapt easily. All of my early training helped me with this new pursuit of mine, and I worked hard at it, and made a success of myself.

The movie of "Barefoot" was very funny and good too, with Jane Fonda and Robert Redford and Charles Boyer. Many of these great old plays became films, and they were frequently very good.

These plays were usually "dinner theater" plays, where the audience would dine first and then sit and watch us go to work. Dinner Theater is a thing of the past I guess. Perhaps it's slowly coming back---I surely hope so because it's a great venue for actors and actresses, and I really loved working that way.

The plays I appeared in were already very famous before I got on board with them, so that didn't hurt. It made it a lot easier. I just truly loved working on stage and think back now and realize how lucky I was to have had that opportunity twice in my lifetime. I'd always thought in my film career that making movies would have to be the most fun, but when I got into my "play period," I found I just loved every minute of it.

Comedies. I worked almost exclusively in comedies. I mean after all, when people go out to a dinner theater they don't want to have a great meal and then settle back to watch some dark tragedy. No. I wanted to make them laugh. Always leave 'em laughing! I did that.

CHAPTER 36

I had worked in three plays with Mike, and they were "Fiorello!," "Tunnel of Love" and "George Washington Slept Here." But you know, Mike just never rehearsed "right." By "right" I mean that during rehearsals, an actor just doesn't "give his all." You play it kind of light, to conserve your energy so you'll be able to go "full bore" for the actual performance. But not Mike. Every rehearsal to him was a performance! I used to tell him to slow down, do it more easily, but he just couldn't. He wouldn't study the script and mark it and plan for things to happen. He just simply charged headfirst into the script, and then drained himself dry when he put on a show like that during rehearsals, when it wasn't necessary. And I really do think because Mike pushed himself like that when it wasn't necessary, that he maybe hastened his own death, although as I've written, there are just so many questions surrounding that whole issue. Well, if it's true what they say about the afterlife, and I do believe in the afterlife, then all of our questions will be answered. Then I'll know.

The other plays I worked in were No, No Nanette, Good News, Hello Dolly, Forty Carats, The Loving Couch, How The Other Half Lives, Cactus Flower, Butterflies are Free, Too Many for the Bed, Under the Yum Yum Tree, The Quilters, Bye Bye Birdie and Janus. What a great experience for me, and best of all, I made over $100,000 doing all those plays! How lucky I was to have gotten those gigs.

I'd also been lucky (and happy) to appear in some plays with Mike, mentioned above, even before our marriage, and we appeared in so many locations. I can't even remember them all; Milwaukee, Chicago, Drury Lane (a theater,) Texas—we went everywhere.

But then I went to Dallas, Texas, to do the "Forty Carats" play which was already very famous. (I'd played the part before I went to Texas to do it.) During the times when I couldn't take the role, it was played by Joan Caulfield. Joan and I looked so much alike when we were younger that we were forever being mistaken for one another. I was already appearing in "Forty Carats," and I do remember one really embarrassing and nasty incident. Some bad mannered and very rude jerk in the audience actually yelled out that I was too old for the part I was playing. Can you imagine anyone doing that sort of thing? How dreadful. Well, I guess he wanted to be heard! I of course went on with the play because I'm a professional and can't let something like that rattle me. But you know, even when terrible things like that happen, you should pay attention to them. I began to think "well, maybe that guy's right," and so I decided to not do the play any longer. However, the producers apparently did not think I was too old for "Forty Carats," and it would run for twelve weeks they told me, and so, I stayed with the play, at least until it had run its course.

CHAPTER 37

Because of what happened with Mike, the trial, his betrayal by the FBI and all the resulting uproar and mess that created, my career was essentially over. I promise I'm not bitter or anything. I loved Mike and stayed with him and nothing could have changed that. It's just the way it was, but I'm so sure I could have kept on acting right up until today. Oh, I got other jobs—I worked in the plays which I mentioned before, and I did do another movie or two, but it was over and I know that's the reason. I mean just because I was getting older was not the reason I didn't work any more. Let's face it, not every single part in a movie belongs to a sweet young thing. I was that sweet young thing for a long time, but I aged, as everyone does, and could have worked in a great many more films. I know this activity of Mike's had a lot to do with the demise of my career.

Mike got into plays for a while, too. But the FBI people were still after him, still kept calling him, even after all he'd been through with them, they still wanted him to do more work for them. Those guys are relentless.

CHAPTER 38

Sometimes I'll look at Mary's wedding album and I can still see how my dear husband Michael O'Shea was ailing then. Something was very, very wrong with him. He was so thin, and so gaunt. I remember how extremely alarmed I'd been. But I never really asked him what was wrong. Maybe I was afraid of the answer. Was it cancer? Was it something else? Was something happening to him that he didn't know about? Was someone doing it to him? I'll never know.

Mike had been alone while I was off doing the plays, and I guess I supposed he just wasn't taking care of himself, not eating properly—or at all. Maybe he'd begun to drink too much, and when people do that, they sometimes don't eat. He'd one time gone to the doctor and had come home with a whole lot of vitamins and things, but nothing seemed to get his health back. I had friends look in on him when I'd be away doing a play, but they never reported anything frightening---just that he spent a lot of time in bed and not enough time eating. Or doing anything, for that matter.

I remember appearing in "No No Nanette" in Chicago and Mike had come there to see me perform. After the show, we went out to have dinner, but he still looked so awful, so terribly thin. He wasn't healthy. His hands were horribly cold. What was happening to my husband? What was coming for Mike? I didn't know. But I was very worried, and it was hard for me to continue on the play circuit with his being so sick, but I had to work.

I hope I do not give the impression I was just off acting in plays to amuse myself, because that was hardly the case. We needed money. And as I've stated before, I had this ingrained work ethic and even if I had not been in show business, I'd still have worked hard all my life. It was natural for me to do that. And besides, if I didn't work, there would be no income. None. I really had no choice, but I am thankful I could work at a job I loved; acting.

I went back to Dallas eventually, to again act in "Forty Carats." The lead in that play had to leave because the part was going to be given to Mike, who came down to Texas in time to do some rehearsing with me. (This didn't seem to hurt that actor's career much. I see him on TV all the time.) It was my plan to spend all my time with Mike, making him eat healthfully, or at least to eat, and to get enough rest, to relax and play. I had so many plans for him, plans to get him healthy again. I really looked forward to our being together in Dallas, working together again. I truly loved being on stage with him. He was a pleasure to act with.

Years before he'd been offered the part of Fiorello La Guardia in the play "Fiorello!" in Meadowbrook, New Jersey. I got the part of his wife, a very small part, but it was good for us. We had a wonderful time together. I know I could have gotten a bigger part, but it required singing, and as you now know, singing is not one of my creative strengths! I well remember our staying at the Plaza hotel so we could go every day to Meadowbrook for the show.

And lo and behold, Mike and I were robbed. At the Plaza of all places! I mean one would think one could be safe at that famous hotel for heaven's sake. They got all my jewelry, my fur stole and Mike's gold watch, too.

I had starred with him in other plays, and the audiences really enjoyed seeing us work together. Mike had a marvelous way of flirting with audiences and getting them to love him. He was an expert at winning over audiences.

We were so happy to learn we'd be working together in "Forty Carats" in Dallas. I was really excited at the prospect. It would be like old times. I could get him healthy again, and we'd hear the applause and life would be good.

How could I know that it would be there that my darling husband would die? I could not, but it is where I lost him, in that apartment in Dallas. He was so young, only sixty-seven, and he died.

The death has always haunted me. Haunted, because I lost the man I loved, but haunted also because of the circumstances. I'll never know if those people who'd snared Mike into doing that spying and other things I'm sure I'll never know about, were somehow implicated in his death. Why was he getting so thin and frail? So physically cold? Were they afraid he knew too much and they had to be rid of him? And if they were responsible for his physical breakdown, how were they doing that? I won't know the answers, ever, but I'll always know the questions.

This is how it happened, how I lost my husband. I'll never forget the night he died. Never. I remember our going to hear the glorious, immortal Mel Torme sing at a restaurant. He came to sit with us to chat for a while after he'd sung to the dinner audience. It was wonderful being there with Mel, one of America's greatest singers. I loved his voice. Who doesn't love the singing of Mel Torme? But alas, at this writing, he's recently died some time after he'd suffered a stroke. I'd read that he kept his passion to once again sing right to the end. I wish he had. Because he's left us forever, our country has suffered an irreplaceable musical loss.

But anyway, it was nice, really sublime being there with Mel and Mike that night, Mike's last night on earth as it turned out. Eventually we became tired and had to leave Mel and go back to our apartment. We had to have our rest for the next day's work. It was a nice apartment, given to us by the play people. It had two bedrooms and I took the smaller one because I'd always liked small bedrooms, and Mike took the larger one so he could put all his luggage in there. Mike always carried a lot of luggage! We prepared to go to sleep. We had rehearsals and play work to do the next morning.

I cannot be sure someone didn't come into the apartment that night, perhaps while Mike was in the bathroom brushing his teeth or something. I was in my bedroom, in bed asleep. I had, and still, have very good ears, and even in my deep sleep, I thought I heard some noise, a . I said to myself "if there's someone in this apartment, I'm not going to wake up. Not now, if they're still here." I was afraid. I didn't want to confront anyone. I would never have gone storming out screaming "Who are you? What do you want?" It felt safer for me to just fake sleep. I pulled the covers up over my head and tried to go back to sleep. But I heard that noise. A strange noise. A noise not usual to that place. A shuffling, clumsy sound, a dragging, like people moving through the hall. Something. I was frightened.

It was in the bathroom I found him the next morning. He was dead, clothed only in his undershorts and lying in the dry bathtub as if he'd toppled into it. It was horrible. I may have screamed. I can't remember. I remember calling some people from the show begging them to please, please come to help me, that my husband was lying in the bathtub and he was dead. They came and so did the police, and I knew I would have to call Mary and tell her this awful news. How could I tell her that her beloved father had died? I dreaded it. I didn't want to tell her. I didn't want her to have to hear that. She'd been married for less than six months, and I had to tell her this terrible news. It was December, 1972. Mike was only sixty-seven, and to this day I cannot shake the feeling that a contract had been put out on his life, considering all he'd gone through before.

Oddly, suddenly in the midst of all this commotion, Mary called. My Mary! She'd had a feeling, a psychic, chilling feeling that something was wrong that morning, so she called. Someone answered and said to her, "Please, wait a moment Mary. Just a minute," and they handed the phone to me. I had to tell her. It was the most awful thing, the hardest thing I've ever had to do. I cannot even remember Mary's reaction, but she seemed to know even before I said those terrible words to her. Mary has always had this gift, and that day, she knew.

Before I could take Mike back to California, there had to be an autopsy, and the cause of death, they said, was heart attack. Mike had been ill. But with what? He had been losing an awful lot of weight, but why? In the last months of his life, my Mike was as cold as death and so very ill, but from what? Heart attack? I wonder. I'll always wonder.

I got him back to California and buried him near Thousand Oaks and no, I do not go back to visit his grave. I also don't believe in sending flowers to gravesites. Terrible people steal flowers today from graves and besides, I'd rather see my money go to a good charity than to a bunch of dead, (or stolen!) flowers. And you know, I don't really believe that people are in those graveyards. Only their shells are. My Mike isn't there. My Michael lives in my heart, with me. Every single day.

The funeral was nice, if one can say that about funerals, and an awful lot of people came to say goodbye to Mike. I still miss him a lot.

CHAPTER 39

I didn't go on with the play right away. I couldn't. I was afraid, I was so tired, and when Mike died, when I found him like that, I realized I had to get back home quickly. I desperately wanted to see Mary and Kent who were living then in our big home in Thousand Oaks.

The memory of that awful time will never leave me. I'd begged Mike to stay away from those terrible things he got involved in. I'd wept, pleaded with him. I'd been frightened all the time. It was awful seeing those strange men always around our home. But he would have never considered not doing these things. He felt it was his patriotic duty to "help out," and so he did. But at what risk? He believed the authorities when they told him he'd never have to testify, but they knew from the start he would have to. He would. Oh, how they lied and lied to him, and lied and lied, and oh, how naïve and trusting he always was. He didn't want his name mentioned publicly because he loved Mary and me and knew we might get hurt if he became known for doing this "work" for the FBI. Mike had been utterly crushed, just shattered to pieces when he found out he'd been betrayed. I hate those people for what they did to my husband. He trusted them so completely, but he was a pawn. He'd been used.

A friend told me that Van Johnson had once said in passing to someone, "Look what they did to Mike O'Shea." I tried for such a long time to get Van on the phone to ask him what he'd meant by that, but he would never take, or return my calls. I simply could not reach him. He obviously knew something and just didn't want to say it to me.

These questions will always torment me. I'm left with these awful, endless lingering doubts about what happened to Mike. The autopsy said "heart attack?" Autopsies can be bought. I'll never have the answers, but I'll always have the doubts and torments.

I might have had the chance though, to ask Van Johnson outright. He was scheduled to appear with me in a show in Texas I did many years after Mike died. It was in 1996 and was called "Follies," not as the main star, but in a good part nonetheless. He came down to Texas before rehearsals even began. Unfortunately, his ego kind of got in the way of things, and he lost the part and so went back to New York.

I well remember Maxine Andrews who was to appear in "Follies" also. She was one of the famous Andrews Sisters singers. It played in Houston and Seattle and was very hard on me—I actually danced (and at 76, that's no easy task, I can tell you. I won't want to do another show like that!)

But one thing annoyed me a lot about Maxine Andrews that I promised to tell you about some chapters back. I've mentioned often that it had always been my habit to rehearse for hours and hours and even more hours before a show opened so that every single move was memorized and "nailed" as they say. But Maxine kept hogging the rehearsal room! I could never get into the room. Well, to be fair it wasn't exactly Maxine's fault. She had a young woman with her---her protector or manager or something--- who would get that room first thing in the morning and would just keep it all day long, so I was never able to adequately rehearse my song and dance number. It nearly drove me crazy! It was infuriating. I do not like to appear on stage or in front of a camera without being thoroughly rehearsed first, to have everything exactly right in my head. It's an old habit and frankly I think it is the only way to be if one is going to be in show business. Oh, this thing with Maxine annoyed me so. But sadly, her poor mind had gotten so fogged that she just couldn't remember the words even though she and that young woman stayed in the rehearsal room for hours and hours every single day, keeping everyone else from using it. Finally they had to put the words on cue cards in the pit for Maxine anyway, so I could have had that room after all.

Well, I'm sorry that happened with Van Johnson and the show, because it was my only chance to ask him the questions I wanted to, but it was not to be.

When I left "Forty Carats" after Mike's death, I told the people I'd be back in two weeks, and so I was. I knew I had to work. I had to have the money, of course, but I also knew I couldn't stand staying home with nothing to do. I had to keep my mind occupied. My brain was whirling with questions, questions that had no answers then, and don't now.

Joan Caulfield, my good and faithful old friend, stepped in for me while I took Mike back home to bury him and to get my life organized. I sent her flowers to thank her when I returned. I had to work, and she understood and graciously gave the part back to me. I wanted to grieve, wanted the time to do that, but my mind was whirling with so many tormenting questions, so it was better for me to get back on that stage.

The play had moved on to Houston by that point. Being on stage again really helped with the grieving process a great deal. It's good to have your mind occupied at a time like that. I really don't know if the audience even knew when the curtain went up and I walked out on stage, that Mike had died just two weeks before. I didn't want to think about that, nor was I interested in a lot of "sympathy applause." I just wanted to put my head down and do the work, and work hard. And that's exactly what I did. I became the character. I am an actress, and that is what we do.

CHAPTER 40

Somewhere in the 1970s I made a film called "Evil Spirits with the remarkable actress Karen Black. I remember it was filmed in a big house and was really fun to do. Every actress or actor should have an opportunity to do a scary film now and again. It really stretches one as an actor.

Actually, Joan Caulfield was given my role in that movie at first, but she called me to ask if I'd like to take this part because she didn't want it. I said I'd love to, that I'd enjoy having this role and would really love to sink my teeth into a horror or suspense film. (Remember, Joan and I were look-alikes.)

The tale of this film was taken from a real-life newspaper story about a woman who took in older people, provided some sort of a rooming house for them, and then stole their Social Security checks. She'd then kill them, after, of course, she got the checks cashed. It was a long time before the police caught up with her.

Karen Black played the role of that woman killer so well. She's a great actress, very sexy and intense. She was always awfully good at those scary roles. I was one of the people who had to get killed in that movie, along with the man who played my husband. Bummer, as they say today!

In the scene where I get killed, I'm brushing my teeth when suddenly, BASH! I get a hatchet in the head. Ugh! I remember coming home to my house in Thousand Oaks, still having fake blood on my head, and badly frightening my poor grandsons.

"Ohhh Grandma!" they cried out. I feel bad about that, and looking back, I should have washed it all out. Those poor kids thought that was pretty horrible.

I really don't know whatever became of "Evil Spirits," and surprisingly, I never saw it on TV. I wish someone would find it and run it. It was a great genre film.

Things were slowing down for me professionally. The plays were drying up and I was finding myself home more and more. I loved to work, but frankly, I found I was kind of enjoying being lazy. I'd worked so hard all

154

my life that kicking back and not doing much really felt sort of good! Little did I know that another phase of my life was about to start, and one I would enjoy very much!

CHAPTER 41

I had arrived at the stage of living where many people, not just professional actors and actresses, ask themselves, "What shall I do with the rest of my life?" I was now getting a pension check from the studios that wasn't exactly huge, but it was enough to live on, if I was careful. So I wasn't poor, and I did have money left over from all the plays I'd done. It was time for me to do something else. I was not ready for the rocking chair and this house does not have a front porch anyway, and even if those things existed, I would not use them!

One day my agent made an odd suggestion. He said I should go on cruises. Cruises? What did he mean? I soon found out. Large cruise lines, such as Royal and others, frequently contact famous people, (not always just from show business) and ask them to join them on a cruise. If they agree, they get to go first class all the way. All the trimmings, and of course they get to go to simply fabulous places, all over the world.

The catch? There is one, but it's not exactly unpleasant. All the cruise directors ask of us, the famous people, is that they hold one really huge group interview, held in the ship's ballroom where all of us would join together and allow everyone attending the "privilege" of asking us all sorts of questions. Anything goes. The directors of the cruise would get in touch with us well before the start of the cruise to find out when it would be convenient for us to speak, (daytime or evening, and what times would be suitable,) and they would also inquire of us what we wanted to discuss with the audiences. I was assured that there were literally no restrictions on what we could discuss.

This sounded just great to me. Imagine, for once we could talk about our feelings, the world's problems, politics and even religion if we wanted to. For once we wouldn't be faced with a barrage of really important questions like, "Do you wear pajamas to bed or do you sleep nude?" Or, "Did you ever have an affair with any of your leading men? And if so, will you please give every possible detail?" That kind of questioning just disgusts me. Those questions are intrusive and rude. Do people who are not in show business have to answer questions like that? They do not, so why is it that

156

when someone is famous they're expected to answer those kinds of personal questions? Don't the famous have any privacy rights as the rest of the world has? I would never ask another person questions like that, and so I expect the same respect to be given to me. Further, I think there are just too many people out there who think that all so-called "movie stars" just sleep around and party all the time, get drunk and do drugs. That's not fair, and it's not true either.

On the cruise ships, we famous folk would have one big evening to answer all the questions asked of us. And surely, I knew there would be the usual "movie star" questions, but at least we could all look forward to some mind-stimulating intelligent questions for a change.

The cruise ship people told us they would expect us to dress up elegantly for that one big evening in front of a large audience. Over the years, I'd accumulated a lot of evening gowns, so I was all set there. They also asked that we mingle with all the passengers daily and during the evenings as the cruise progressed, and if possible answer even more of their questions. That was fine with me. I was beginning to get really excited about all of this.

Thus, knowing everything about what would be expected of me, I pondered about taking those cruises for about one minute and then agreed. It sounded like great fun and it would be a way for me to see a lot of the world and to do it for free. I couldn't wait to begin.

These cruises, for which we were not paid because technically we were not entertaining, began late in the 1970s, and I remember them with pleasure. Many famous people went on the same cruises I went on. Esther Williams, June Allyson, Margaret O'Brien, Ann Miller, Virginia O'Brien,--- oh, so many others. Men too. We had, as they say, a ball!

It turned out that the cruise directors weren't really too strict about our mingling with the guests. I didn't much care to do that after all, and more wanted to spend my time in the ship's library, walking the decks or even going to bed early to get a good night's rest, something I had always been able to do and always liked to do.

But not June Allyson! She could mingle forever! I've never known anyone so adaptable. She remains the darling, sweet woman she portrayed in her films. No wonder she played those roles so well---she was playing the real June Allyson.

Junie loved to get all gussied up and walk around the boat talking to every single person she could. And everyone crowded around her like bees on a honeypot. It was really funny to watch that happening. The elegant, swellegant Esther Williams was maybe a bit more reticent, but she mingled too, and she always looked just simply smashing, not so much different from her days as one of the most famous movie stars in the world. All that swimming didn't harm her any; her face and figure remain exquisite. She and June have really held it together and don't look much different from the days when they were so famous in the movies.

I'll never forget when we landed in Spain during one of the cruises. There were so many people there and all of them were shouting my name! Virginia Mayo! Virginia Mayo! Over and over. I hadn't known I had fans there, and it was simply thrilling to me to have that happen.

We had wonderful times on those cruises. In all I must have gone on a dozen or more, I can't really remember the exact total, but they went on until the late 1980s.

In the late 70s, however, I went back to Ireland to do a play. I had hesitated at first because I was worried it would bring back sad memories of my time there with Mary and Mike, but it didn't. I'd been asked to appear in a play called "Who Gets the Drapes?" It was very funny, but they didn't give any of us enough time to rehearse, and as I may have mentioned already, I'm really pretty much of a stickler about getting enough rehearsal time! And, there were other problems. One of the actors was Irish American who took it upon himself to move all over the stage all the time, completely upsetting everyone. He also talked too loudly, and stepped on everyone's lines. I guess he was determined to steal the show from the rest of us. It was very annoying. But the show went for a few weeks, although one of the actors I had to work with had really rotten teeth which was completely gross. But it did force me to bring out all my acting skills! Ugh. I hated having to act opposite that guy.

They told us there were ghosts upstairs in that theater. It was very curious and odd, and sometimes I really thought I could sense their presence!

158

CHAPTER 42

Television did figure into my life – at least a little. I guess I don't recall too much about being on TV because it wasn't my favorite thing to do. I'd get paid, but not much, and it wasn't my favorite kind of acting, although sometimes I didn't have to act.

The talk shows were kind of fun though. I was thrilled when I got asked to be on The Dinah Shore Show because as you may recall from the beginning of this book, we'd shared a dressing room way, way back in the vaudeville days, and I'd liked her so much then. I was really looking forward to being on her show. Honestly she was a classy lady, a great golfer and as nice as she could possibly be. Everything nice that's said about her is true.

But alas, the day I was to appear on her show, Dinah was on vacation or something. The show was to be hosted by Robert Klein, but even though I was disappointed, he was really great. He'd actually asked to speak with me on that show, and so I was honored. He's so talented, funny and brilliant. A fabulous mind. We had a great time together that day.

I remember only a little about my appearance in a show called "Night Gallery." I played opposite Patty Duke and I had to jump out of a window and land on a street. That's all I can come up with!

I remember having to fly to Cleveland to appear on the old Mike Douglas Show. What a nice guy. I felt terrible when he lost his show. He was so funny and decent and what a good singer he was. Who makes these decisions, anyway? What a loss to the viewing audience it was when he had to leave.

"Remington Steele." Now that guy isn't too hard to look at; Pierce Brosnan. Dorothy Lamour was on that show playing herself. I was on the show playing myself too. What fun that was! I truly enjoyed playing Virginia Mayo, and as I recall, I "got her down" pretty good! I didn't get to sing or dance on that show—it was one of those silly "catch the bad guys" kinds of show, but great fun to do and it was such a kick playing me!! Eerie in a lot of ways, gives one an odd feeling, but it was something I would have regretted missing.

I did an appearance on Angela Lansbury's show "Murder She Wrote." Now there's a woman with great staying power. She's been acting since when? The 1930s? Forties? Remember her in "Gaslight" with the smooth, slick, gorgeous Charles Boyer? And remember that wonderful actress Ingrid Bergman in that movie? (I think she won an award for her role in that.) I've read that Charles was so short he had to stand on a box a lot, and Angela was so tall she couldn't play opposite him unless for sure he was up on that box!

And let us never forget my old friend Lloyd Nolan. He played himself on "Remington Steele" and was the kind of actor who could, and would, take on any role.

And of course, "The Love Boat." Everyone does (or did) "The Love Boat." I was no exception! And everyone wanted to be on that show too, so it wasn't always easy to get a spot. My agent told me to go directly to Aaron Spelling and ask him if I could appear on it, that I should tell him I'd been on the road so much I had been unavailable. That I should insist I get a part. That's what happened. Mr. Spelling said yes, he'd also been wanting me to be on the show, and so they gave me a part in one episode. I remember Mr. Spelling's asking me how much money I wanted, and I answered, "I surely don't know. Why don't you just give me what you give all the other actors?" So that's what he did. Aaron Spelling is a really wonderful man and the entertainment he's given to the world can't be matched.

I did work briefly on a soap opera called "Santa Barbara" but I just wasn't right for the part, shouldn't have done it, so enough said about that.

I also worked on "Police Story," "The Outsider," a few Bob Hope Specials, "Daktari," "AM New York," "Castle of Evil," "Lannigan's Rabbi," and "The Merv Griffin Show." I've also done so many interviews, I can't even count them. I'm still asked to appear on the radio and TV occasionally. People love to have a look at an old former movie diva, and I don't mind obliging them!

CHAPTER 43

Before this book ends, I'd really like to talk a bit about my beloved family. I've kind of touched on them, but I'll say a little more now.

Mary met Kent here in California, and looking back at their older photos, I will say they were kind of hippy-ish. But I wasn't terribly concerned about all of that. I understood it was a phase and that they'd grow out of it. I think Kent at first had a big fuzzy hairdo and then a long ponytail. It was in the ponytail phase when I first met him. (Quite a contrast to his today's haircut which is so close and neat he looks like a marine. Or a cop. Which he is!)

They met at a church dance and they were both only about fifteen and sixteen. I think they fell in love instantly and truly, they've stayed that way. The first time I met him I liked him. They'd sit on the front lawn of our home here in Thousand Oaks and they'd talk and talk. Mike liked Kent too, very much, and was pleased that his beloved daughter would marry him.

They went to Colorado to kind of "test out" their love, and they got married there in the first of their weddings, (this one in a church, Lutheran.) I flew in from Chicago where I was appearing in "No No Nanette" and attended their big wedding. People—not Mike or I—told them they were too young, but they didn't listen. And I'm glad they didn't, because the years have proved that they were right and those people warning them were wrong. They have stayed married all these years and will remain married to each other until the end.

Mike and I asked Mary and Kent to come back to Thousand Oaks to live with us, and they did. Neither of them had jobs, so Kent amazed us all by saying he'd decided to become a police officer, (now he's a Deputy Sheriff) and he's very, very good at it. I wish Mike had seen Kent succeed at this. He'd have been so very proud, his loving police business as he did. I don't know if Mike ever talked with Kent about his "secret" passion for police work, or if he influenced him in any way, but today Kent is very comfortable with his choice. And from all reports, he's good at what he does.

Kent studied and studied all night long after his long hard hours of being a chef, learning everything about police work from piles and piles of books. He passed all his exams, and graduated. We all went to that ceremony somewhere in Ventura and oh didn't those young men look glorious in their dress uniforms. Floyd and Delores were there too. It was a great experience.

First came Lucas, and then Evan and finally Dillon. All three boys were born within a few years of each other. Honestly I think those boys are as different as they can be. I see similarities but most people think they're not even related! They're great kids and I love them madly and can't imagine my life without them in it.

Mary turned out to be the most devoted mother. I hadn't had any doubts about that, but still it was amazing to see her mothering those boys. She seemed born to do it. A natural. They are very close, even today, and discuss everything together and Mary and Kent spend a lot of time with the kids, something I hear is not that common today.

Mary decided that she wanted to home-school her kids, and so she did just that. As a matter of fact, she became so good at it, her school expanded to such a degree that in time she had to leave it because it had become too ponderous for her to handle. And besides, the boys were finished with their education. Lucas eventually went to regular public school and was (and still is) very involved in sports.

I remember so well when Lucas was tiny and it was my job to keep his mind off of where his mommy was, if she'd had to go out. I'd dance for him and make funny faces and he'd laugh and play with me. It was wonderful.

Mary always wanted to be an at-home mother and she and Kent arranged it so she could do that. They both thought being with their children was the most important thing there was on earth, and so they made sure someone was at home all the time. No one ever seemed to want to be in show business, at least when the boys were small. Mary most of all! She used to get so nervous when she saw me in a play, worried I'd forget my lines. And of all three boys, I'd supposed Lucas would be an actor because of his extreme outgoing personality. He works hard and plays hard at sports, in particular ice hockey at which he's apparently very good.

Dillon expresses an interest in acting and is, at this point, doing a lot of writing of scripts. He's very funny and sensitive. A real thinker. He may go into the business and has seen some success in small acting roles. He apparently likes doing that.

Evan I think probably would rather write than act, if he had to make that choice. He's witty and wry and I think a deep thinker too, and I suspect

162

in time we'll see something just go BOOM with Evan, when he decides to channel his remarkable abilities in one direction.

It's funny the memories that stick with a person. I remember coming back home after a long, exhausting play run and not finding anyone around. I went upstairs and there was the whole family, all five, snuggled into Mary and Kent's big king-sized bed. It looked wonderful and warmed my heart to see that. Oh, this family of mine has given me so much joy.

I remember Lucas as a baby. He would always wake up a few hours after he'd been asleep and begin to cry and so Mary would put him in their bed. Then the other two would want the same thing and so they'd join them. Mary and Kent had read that in a lot of countries they do that with their children, having them sleep in the same bed, and that it's healthy and good. In time, kids don't want to do that any more and so they stop on their own and go back into their own beds. It sure didn't hurt the Johnston boys! Today they are so close to their parents and as I've said before, they seem to talk endlessly on any subject and Mary and Kent always stop everything to listen to them and advise them. I think Mary and Kent would be perfectly happy if those boys stayed right home with them until they married. Or even after. They wouldn't mind having their son's wives come to live with them! This is a very tight family.

One very interesting thing about Mary is that while she wants her boys to be near her for as long as possible, she and Kent are not clingy. I mean they encourage the boys to go out with as many friends as they want to (and oh! Do they ever have friends!) and to have as many young people as possible come over to the house. I hear young people running upstairs to the boys' bedrooms so often I don't even bother to look up any longer. The front door is always opening and closing at our house and the sounds of young people laughing and talking seems to go on until late every night. It's such a good thing. The kids who come here all seem to be so directed, so focused. I don't see any indication of drunkenness or drug use. I don't hear them cussing or screaming and they don't even really blast the music. Maybe I live in a dream world, but I don't think so. Lucas and Evan and Dillon are big, sweet clean-cut young men and that's the sort of young people they attract. This whole thing is a joy to me.

Dillon was born in Thousand Oaks, but his two brothers were born in a hospital elsewhere and their doctor was the same man who'd delivered their mother, my Mary. A great doctor and a wonderful coincidence!

One time Kent went to some place, I forget where, to learn about Martial Arts and became so interested in it that he now has a thriving Martial Arts business, only it's not a business. He teaches it once a week to a bunch of very dedicated people and he doesn't charge them for his time or knowledge. Kent is a man interested in doing good in this world, and this is one way he does it. He teaches people who want to know how to protect themselves in this world and he himself is very good at it too. Kent works so hard at this and is working toward earning his own belts too. I do admire him a lot.

And so having them all here with me has always been my greatest joy. I don't know what my life would be like if they weren't here. Mary takes such good care of me. Do we squabble? You bet. A lot! But there is an underlying love between us that can never change. Never.

CHAPTER 44

I wonder, sometimes, if people think that because those of us who have been privileged to act in films for a number of years, and aren't seen any longer in current movies, if they think we just hide in the attic surrounded by our clippings and posters and weep a lot. Hardly! I still live in this big house that Mike and I built in Thousand Oaks, a home I love, and it is just alive with friends and people and kids and dogs. Always dogs! There is never a dull moment around here and I feel just simply surrounded with love and happiness and fun.

I guess I know there are movie folk out there who are past their so-called "greatness," and perhaps they do sit around like Norma Desmond watching old films, getting drunk, smoking, weeping, licking their so-called "wounds"----whatever. Not I! I have great memories of my past years and don't dwell on them in a negative way. They were fun times. Times not many get to have. I keep saying it and I apologize for repeating it, but I've been so blessed. So very blessed!

And I do keep busy. I'm not sitting on my front porch in a rocking chair and furthermore I don't own a rocking chair OR a front porch! I keep in touch with many old friends, both in and out of show business. I don't drink the way some of my acting colleagues did and do. Never got into it (made me so dizzy) and so I don't sit on that non-existent rocking chair with a Bourbon in my hand. Don't swear, don't smoke—never did, although I had to fake it in some movies. (And I really didn't inhale!) I think my only vice now is chocolate, and my daughter keeps sneaking it away from me and hiding it when someone gives me a box. (But I'll always find it. Always!)

The list of famous and interesting people I've met and known over the years is so long. I know I shouldn't even be making this list---I'm fearful of leaving someone out who's important, but here are some, and I hope you'll bear with me. I do want to say up front here that I perhaps didn't know all of the following people, but I've put in some names of actors and actresses whose work I've admired and loved, and so if wishing I could know them would make me know them, then I'd know them! (That makes sense to me. Hope it does to you, too!)

And so I'd like to talk in this chapter about these people I've met, at least as many as I can remember, and how they may or may not have influenced me. Some I never met, but I have opinions on all of them, and many of them influenced my career in a lot of ways. Some I loved, some I definitely did not!

I have been so fortunate in my life to meet so many well-known people, and not all were in show business. (And come to think of it not all were well known!) I've met scientists and inventors, authors, great painters and sculptors. Show business has given much to me, and part of it is that I've been able to be in the vicinity of a lot of people who have shaped the thinking of a lot of other people.

And maybe in some ways I do sit with my memories, but it's not morbid or sad for me to do that. Memories can be such great things, and even though I'm a busy woman today, I love to take the time to remember. I smile when I think of some of the things I got to do, and oh, the people I've met. The people! Some I knew very briefly, some I knew for years and years. Like Rhonda Fleming and June Allyson, Patty Andrews. Dear Jane Russell, the splendid and beautiful Kathryn Grayson, still a friend. I can remember my friendship with Ginger Rogers. I never met Fred Astaire, but Ginger and I were friends. She was just wonderful, such a versatile actress and she couldn't have been nicer. Her mother was a tremendous influence on her life, you know, guiding her and being her companion.

I remember going to Ginger's house one day up in Oregon. We arrived unexpectedly, and Ginger wasn't home, but her mother was, and she showed us all through the house, and it was lovely. I got to see Ginger at a number of parties in the last years of her life, and I talked with her whenever I could because I knew she was ill and wouldn't last too much longer. At the end, she was in a wheelchair, which was terrible, to see---that graceful, athletic most beautiful woman, that dancer with the glorious, supple body, being forced to sit in a wheelchair. She died peacefully, they tell me and I was relieved and happy to hear that.

And Laraine Day, Anne Jeffreys, Margaret Lindsay, Ralph Bellamy, Harriet Hilliard Nelson, (she goes way, way back, from "the act" days!) Susan Strasberg, Janet Leigh, Jane Wyatt, Lizabeth Scott, Joel McRea, Dorothy McGuire, Rudy Vallee (not my favorite person, not many people's favorite person for that matter,) Guy Madison. Evelyn Keyes. I just saw her recently, at a party. (I do go to parties a lot, when I can and if they sound interesting.) She was married to Artie Shaw (so were a lot of other women,) and she's very bright. She's written a couple of books. She was married a lot too, and even wrote about that.

And I remember the indomitable Thelma Ritter, oh what a funny woman, Jerry Lewis, Vivaca Lynfors, Ronald Reagan, a man I liked very much, who always, even when he was President, treated me with great deference. We had a wonderful time making "She's Working Her Way Through College," (still my favorite film) and "The Girl From Jones Beach." John Agar, a nice man, married for a while to Shirley Temple. His best friend was John "Duke" Wayne and they worked in films together. Ronald Coleman. (Oh, that voice of his.) The beautiful, mega-talented Diana Lynn. The razzle dazzle Shirley Mac Laine. I sat near her when she was pregnant with her first and only child, a daughter who's an actress now. Is her name "Sashi"? I remember how she talked and talked and talked and she was so very cute. Bubbly. Gamin-like. Just adorable. Wonderful author. Fabulous dancer. We still nod to one another now. We never got to be great pals, I'm sorry to say.

Karl Malden, another great actor. Mae West. Well, I didn't ever meet her, but don't forget that she threw me out of her apartment when she found out I had dogs! Tab Hunter, Wallace Beery, (I wish I'd met him,) Jack Carson who was at Warner Brothers and a nice man. Acted in a lot of movies! Great jaw muscle action to show emotion. Adolph Menjou—I met him on the street once. He was a staunch Republican and was a very dapper dresser. (Won Best Dressed Man award year after year.) George Raft? Well, I've already explained about him! He claims he put up his own money to get me into his movie "Red Light." I wonder. I wish I'd known Norma Shearer. Peter Lorre, oh, what a wonderful gentleman he was, at least that's what I always heard. I wish I'd met him. A sweet man, I'm told. Frank Lovejoy, a good man, great actor. Bette Davis. (I've already told you about her! What a snob! She acted like she was a queen or something. Heck, no queen would ever be as rude as she was.) Remember that line "Every time he kisses me I wipe my mouth!" Very Bette Davis thing to say! Joan Crawford. I really didn't know her but I was always frankly sort of put off by those huge lips and huger shoulders. I guess those things became her trademark. I mean she was hardly an unpopular actress, but it seemed to be too stylized for me. The elegant Randolph Scott, a southerner. Very much the gentleman. Gallant! Married a rich lady. Raymond Massey, Charlton Heston, two men who were pompous----well, you know. Andrew Duggan, an actor who went on forever. Marilyn Maxwell. Ethel Merman. Never met her but wow, could she perform. I used to think you hadn't seen anything until you'd seen and heard Ethel Merman! I can still hear her belting out "Everything's Comin' Up Roses" from "Gypsy." Vera Ellen, my dear, darling friend. She was at Mike's and my wedding. And, she could dance like no other woman alive. Energy? She invented the word. She died far too young, you know. Her baby had died of SIDS, and that horrible experience so affected my dear friend, she just simply lost her will to live. She thought there was nothing to live for. The Gishes---didn't know them, but they were like China dolls. John Mills? I was with him in the line-up to meet the Royalty way back when. Mamie Van Doren. She was so cute and a good friend of mine. Very sexy and funny and talented. But Jayne Mansfield was a freak and that's all I have to say about that. Ann-Margret—I reserve judgment about her because I think she fakes her singing and dancing and isn't much of an actress. Henry Fonda. Didn't like him. Sorry, but I thought he was a jerk. Vincent Price was a great man, author, cook, and art collector. What a great guy! Yes. And Charlton Heston made a great (and lasting) Planet of the Apes film, and of course was awfully good at being God and Moses etc. Boris Karloff was in The Secret Life of Walter Mitty with me and he was very good. I don't think anyone knows he was in that movie. He played a psychiatrist and he was great. He was kind and gentle and sweet. Ed Wynn. Keenan Wynn. I knew Ray Bolger slightly, Mr. Rubber Legs! Jack Haley. Johnny Weismueller. Great swimmer. Great yeller. The wonderful Ann Miller. Jane Powell—I see her every once in a while. She's still so nice. Martha Raye. I wonder sometimes about that marriage of hers at the end of her life. Well, maybe she was lonely. Margaret O'Brien who still acts and as you now know, appeared with me in Barefoot. We're still very good friends. Richard Widmark. Remember his crazy laugh in the early years? James Dean. Sal Mineo—didn't know him. He was stabbed to death, poor kid. Frederick March appeared with me in "The Best Years of our Lives." Dana Andrews was dear to me. An alcoholic. Wonderful Teresa Wright is still around. Myrna Loy, oh boy, so beautiful. Cathy O'Donnell was lovely and tender. We went to Mexico once. Didn't know Marlena Dietrich. Robert Mitchum, the perfect bad boy! Edward Arnold—a marvelous radio personality before he went into films. Pat O'Brien. Mildred Natwick. I think she appeared in one of the productions of Barefoot in the Park, but I never met her. Audie Murphy. I never met that man, but I think so very much of him. I saw all of his movies and the movie of his life. He was turned down at West Point because of some sort of hip injury from the war, you know. And no one can get in there if they're "flawed." It was heartbreaking to him, and he was a war hero! I don't understand why people, especially people in Hollywood, didn't rave more about him. He was a believable actor and let's face it, it takes a lot to become a movie star. But most importantly, he was a true war hero and we can surely use a lot of them! He just didn't seem to get the recognition he deserved, as far as I was concerned. Lucille Ball—I knew her vaguely. Never did like that awful "I Love Lucy" TV show. Not funny. I knew Edie Adams—remember her? She'd been married to Ernie Kovacs—and Lucy made Edie change her hairdo three times so it wouldn't look better than Lucy's on a show they did together. Lucy was so heavy-handed. And frankly, I never thought her TV show was in the least bit funny. Sorry America! Jean Peters. Well, she got the prize, didn't she? Howard Hughes! Sophia Loren? What a lucky woman to have a husband who knew enough about the business to pick out all her films and make her the star he did. I'm sure she's had her face fixed a lot because he probably told her to, but she is a stunning beauty still. (I hate that. All the rest of the actress have to sort of forge ahead on our own without a big-name husband to push us and a lot of plastic surgery to "improve" us. Doris Day had great managers behind her, getting her all the good studios and good parts, while the rest of the actors and actresses had to do it on our own. Zazu Pitts. Wonderful the way she used her hands. Mickey Rooney. (Don't ask.) Guy Madison. Dear man. Rosalind Russell, a woman I never really knew, but I did admire her acting abilities. John Wayne—I really didn't care much for him. Didn't know him very well. He liked to marry dark-haired women. Wendell Corey was OK. I always thought he looked moldy. Van Heflin, good actor. George Sanders—tragic death. I mean to commit suicide because you're bored? That can be fixed, after all. We can all find something to do in this life. There's so much out there! But a lovely, wonderful voice and a funny brilliant man. Married Zsa Zsa Gabor. Cary Grant—a rue! Wonderful leading man. Wish I'd known him. What a glorious, elegant man. Nothing much he wouldn't tackle and do well. Suzanne Pleshette. Didn't know her, but a real good actress. Eleanor Powell. Zachary Scott---hmm—well, a good actor. Ann Sheridan. Billie Burke was just wonderful. Funny lady. Loretta Young—how beautiful and smart. Broderick Crawford, a very good actor, stylized, did his dialogue too quickly to suit me. Shelley Winters—that voice! Kind of overdoes it, but she's a great actress too. Elvis Presley---I actually met him too! Never did go for his music. He can't much sing, but wiggles a lot. All the girls think he's cute. Sexy. Oh no. I mean if you want to hear great singers, take a listen to Vic Damone and Mel Torme and Frank Sinatra and Tony Bennett and Jack Jones and of course all the songs written by the Gershwins and Cole Porter and Sammy Kahn and Irving Berlin and all the rest of them from that era. Don't get me started on today's so called "music!" Being a dancer and (dubbed!) singer, I got to hear and perform the best in America's music. I love great music. Today's "music" is not only not great it's not music! Steve McQueen was so cute and funny. Good actor. Terrific. Tony Randall. Does comedy really well. Red Skelton—I worked with him in Vaudeville. He used to do an act and would rehearse it in a restaurant. Completely uninhibited man! He'd begun in the Muny Opera. (St. Louis has a lot of famous people born there. We're very proud of our city!) Ann Sothern. Rod Steiger—wasn't he good? Terribly tense guy. Those gorgeous men Burt Reynolds and Tom Selleck. Wow! Brian Dunleavy—he had to wear built up shoes! short man and back then it was necessary that men be taller—and older—than women are. Thank heavens that old and silly rule doesn't exist any longer! Margaret Sullavan. Well, I think she was a little wacky. She was so melodramatic and her speaking voice always sounded as if she was about to burst into tears! Hammy. Yvonne De Carlo—good actress but kind of weird! Franchot Tone. I had a friend who used to date him. He was married a whole lot of times! Gary Cooper—I told you about him at the start of my book. Olivia de Havilland—glorious actress. Lives in France, I think. Robert Walker—only met him. And I love Robert Wagner. What a nice man and good actor. Tony Martin. His voice is still great even though he's so much older. Vivien Leigh. Clifton Webb—wish I'd known him. Orson Wells. Jane Withers. She used to be the darling of Hollywood and still is. Everyone likes her. Remember Roland Young in those Topper things? Great character actor. John Barrymore and Lionel and Eleanor. Were they crazy? Well, they were all alcoholics and now Drew has her troubles but I think she's straightening out and she most definitely is becoming a very fine actress. Dan Dailey. I wish I'd known him because he was a loose and jazzy dancer and a good actor and singer, but I never had the pleasure. Robert Cummings—so good in comedy. Stayed looking young for a long time because he took a thousand pills a day! Jeannie Crain—she could do everything. Gene Tierney—classic looks. Dick Haymes used to beat up Rita Hayworth I hear, when they were married. Jan Sterling was married to Broderick Crawford. Marilyn Monroe. I didn't know her, but of course knew her first husband well, Jim Dougherty, who is still my dear friend. Gilbert Roland—so Mexican, so handsome! Irene Dunne, just the best. Wonderful in "Life with Father." Peter Lawford. Deborah Kerr. I was jealous of her because she got all those good roles. Frankly I get a little annoyed at all those British women who come over here and take away the roles from us just because they've got an English accent. Just because someone is British doesn't mean they're better. Pier Angeli. Michael Rennie—I adored his work. Errol Flynn—what can anyone say about that bounder! Walter Brennan—that man won three Oscars with Sam Goldwyn. Walter Pigeon. Such a sweet nice man and of course treated me with such kindness when I got so sick on that Howard Hughes plane going to New York. Cornel Wilde—I went on one of the cruises with him and shortly after that, I went to his funeral. Gorgeous man. Richard Burton. Dorothy McGuire—went on a cruise with her. What a beautiful face. Gregory Peck, -- who doesn't love that classy guy? Robert Redford. Isn't he darling? Even his wrinkles are real pretty. Jane Wyman—Ronnie Reagan's wife for a while. Wonderful in Johnny Belinda for which she won the Academy Award and never uttered a word! Lee Remick, a darling woman. Died way too young. Debbie Reynolds—another woman with great staying power! I love her dearly. Stage and movies—she's marvelous. She is just so funny and is a great mimic. Debbie has a very witty mind. Stewart Granger. Barbara Stanwyck? Well, I hate her. She was always

170

after all her leading men and even went after Mike when they worked in "The Lady of Burlesque." How obnoxious. A very critical actress. Everyone talks about how wonderful she was, but I know different. She was married to Robert Taylor for a while, but they divorced. The most ugly actress that ever got anyplace. Bad figure. Flat chested. Am I angry? Yeah, because she kept going after my husband. George Hamilton. Very connected to the Philippines and Imelda Marcos, through his beloved mother. And speaking of Imelda, I went to the Philippines one time after Mike died. It was in the 1970s and I went because my publicist Dale Olsen told me it would be a good idea to go, that it was important for me to get around and be seen a lot. There was a film festival going on down there and he thought it would be a perfect time to go. Oh what a long trip that was, changing planes in Japan and all. But go I did. I'd gone with my dear old friend, white haired Lee Graham who has since died. He was dear to me and I loved him a lot. Anyway, we stayed at the Manila Hotel, and I think I may have attended one film. One afternoon I was at a party being thrown by Imelda Marcos. Of course, as was everything she did, it was a fabulous affair, and yes, she sang at the party as she always did. Her husband Ferdinand hadn't yet begun his troubles and he was there too, but always in another room, so I didn't get to see much of him. George Hamilton was there, of course, with his fabulous mother. Alexis Smith was there. (I remember one day Imelda announced that she wanted everyone to be at the waterfront the next morning, early, so she could take us all out on her enormous yacht. I'd spent the night vomiting because the water made everyone sick. We all complained, but then we all got well. I put on what I thought would be play clothes, you know, yacht clothing, slacks and a shirt. We all boarded and I was horrified to see Imelda getting on board in a fabulous silk gown. Oh my. Well, I was just Virginia Jones from Missouri. What did I know??!! Imelda had even assigned a woman to follow me around to make sure I was comfortable and taken care of. Can you imagine the cost of all this? It was a country of such wealth and such horrific poverty. I'll never forget it. And the food at that party on the yacht! HUGE bowls of caviar, tables everywhere with yet another gigantic bowl of caviar on each of them. We all ate and ate and ate and Imelda then went off to put on another fabulous gown. She changed her gowns a lot during parties! One of the Ford women was there. What a crowd! And a full orchestra! We all got off the yacht in Corridor! Well anyway, back to the party on land. I happened to see Robert Duvall. I'd always greatly admired his work and so I walked across the lawn toward him, and introduced myself and told him that I'd been a great admirer of his for a long time. That man stared down at me, and turned and walked away. He just walked away from me! Is that the rudest thing you've ever heard? I was left standing there. Oh, it was terrible. What a horrible thing to do. I was so mortified, having to stand there alone like that. Why is he like that? Well, I guess something happens to people when they achieve great fame; they perhaps decide that they do not have to have manners any longer.

Back to business. I loved Edward G. Robinson. Jason Robards Jr., Cliff Robertson. He's on the edge of the big social circle because of his former marriage to the wealthy Dina Merrill, who became a credible actress herself and is still working. Cliff was a good actor who had principals and blew the whistle on that big Hollywood guy for cheating him and others out of some money, I think, and then didn't get any work for a long time. I hope he's OK now. He should have been rewarded for what he did, but no. He got himself ostracized. The guy he told on of course is right back in business as if nothing happened. Van Johnson—likes everyone to know he's around! I never worked with him however. Hoagie Carmichael---met him but didn't know him but of course he's the best. He left us a huge body of fabulous music. I recently sat between Bob and Delores Hope at a luncheon and was saddened to see how old Bob has become. Well, after all, he's in hid mid nineties now, so it must be hard for him to partake in conversations. When I went to Dorothy Lamour's funeral he came with Delores. They came in a side door, and I'm glad he came up, because after all, Dorothy was wonderful in his "on the road" films. Lon Chaney Jr. Eve Arden is the one person I truly hated in Hollywood. She was such a snob and everyone was beneath her. I remember one time standing right next to Eve and Danny Kaye. They began to talk and ignored me, until Eve said in a loud voice to Danny; "Don't you hate to be around people who just can't do anything?" Obviously, she was talking about me. He agreed with her and they went on talking about me with me standing right there. She was such a bitch. She must have been referring to the fact that I had to get a double to do my singing, like that's some kind of sin or something. I never pretended it was I who was singing. Dubbing was commonplace, and after all, I did everything else myself. I remember having to be on one of the cruises with her and during the big gathering I said some very funny things and got the passengers to laugh. Eve sat there with a simpering smile and later on said, "Oh Virginia, you were VERY cute." Sure. She meant that! The Andrews Sisters—I got to be good friends with all of them, Maxine, Laverne and Patty, and Patty is still here and we're friends and talk all the time. Don Ameche. I never worked with him. He was with Fox forever. Eddie Albert is still kicking. Anthony Quinn. Caesar Romero was so nice, gay, elegant. Great, and kind to women. Errol Flynn was introduced to me in my dressing room one time. Alice Faye was a wonderful lady, married to Phil Harris. They were great together. I think Phil was a Native American. Greta Garbo. Didn't know her but liked her. I bumped into her in New York City one time. I stopped to look in a store window and there she was, standing right

172

next to me. Greta Garbo! And SHE was looking at ME! Wow. So I looked at HER! We stared and moved on. I knew if I spoke, she'd run away. So I kept silent. The beautiful, gracious Maureen O'Hara. Betty Garrett, one of my all time favorites! I saw her at a party recently and called to her and we talked. She suffered so much because her husband Larry Parks was investigated by Joe McCarthy and was accused of being a communist. Because of that, he never worked much after he made The Al Jolson Story (Jolson sang all his own songs.) Ann Rutherford. Farley Granger, one of Hollywood's Golden Boys. Not terribly talented except for the movie he made with Robert Walker. Gloria Grahame. Didn't ever seem to move her upper lip much, but was very funny in Oklahoma with my beloved friend Gene Nelson, a man I miss so much. What a dancer. Kathryn Grayson—so beautiful, and that voice! We're still in touch. Her brother went to high school with me. He once played the lead in "The Taming of the Shrew," where I played Bianca. I called Katherine and told her I had this photo of the whole cast from way back then, and she was thrilled and asked me to mail it to her, that she'd copy and return it. She's so lovely and sweet. Patricia Neal, a fabulous woman. I admire her enormously. Mercedes McCambridge. She could play the most ominous roles! Spencer Tracy, one of the world's greatest actors, but he could be a drunken thug, beating up innocent people and destroying property all over the place. He had a lot of problems but his long almost-three decade long love affair with Katharine Hepburn helped him stay focused to a large degree. Paul Henried, wish I'd known him. Audrey Hepburn—I did meet her once. Beautiful. Skinny. Linda Darnell was so beautiful. She tried to do plays too, but had trouble with lines. She couldn't cope with them. Died in a fire. Gruesome. Dorothy Lamour. I went to her funeral. I remembered when three of us were picked to play in a Remington Steele. It was me playing me, Lloyd Nolan and Dorothy Lamour. A show written for three of us especially. Roy Rogers and Dale Evans—good people and were wonderful to children. Very Christian. Barry Fitzgerald. Fernando Lamas, married to Esther Williams. Very Latin traditional marriage—Esther was there to take care of him, and she seemed happy to do it. I had to kiss him once in a movie and I hated it. He wasn't so good at it! Esther has remarried. She and I have remained friends and as I've already noted in this book, I think she is a brilliant businesswoman. She is in complete control of her career. No one can even run a film clip of her without paying her. Tyrone Power. Brian Keith and I appeared in a movie together. He was just so good. And then he committed suicide. Why? How terrible. Norman Rockwell. I got to meet that great artist. I love to paint and I think I'm pretty good at it, but he was a genius. Nina Foch. Joan Fontaine. In a book she wrote she said I once tried out for a part that she got. Well, that must have been a real trick because I hadn't even arrived in Hollywood yet. Glenn

Ford. Kind of a lech. Keeps pictures of himself all over his house. John Garfield. Wasn't he wonderful? Never knew him but wish I had. Gena Rolands and John Casavettes. Kay Francis. Sort of weird. Bob Fosse—think of what he contributed to the dance in this country. William Powell. Wasn't he wonderful? Funny. Smart-allecky! Jackie Cooper—another stayer in the business. Charles Coburn—didn't know him but loved his work. Jean Simmons—wasn't she beautiful? Still is. Zsa Zsa Gabor. I met all the Gabors, Zsa Zsa, Eva and Magda although Magda mostly stayed in Palm Springs. However, I never did meet the infamous Mama. Robert Taylor—the world's heart throb. Didn't age well. Ruth Roman, a lovely woman, great actress. Alexis Smith, Kim Novak. (Not much to say about her.) Jimmy Stewart—the best. Just the best. Merle Oberon, part East Indian (a big dark secret for her,) and very beautiful. Married for a while to the famous producer/director Alex Korda. Merv Griffin—he had me on his show. Great interviewer. I remember telling him on one of his shows that I recalled how he was originally thought of as a threat to Gordon MacRae when he first began in movies and he looked really angry at that. (I thought I was complimenting him.) But he never had a voice the caliber of MacRae's. Griffin is very, very wealthy. Herbert Marshall--I wonder if everyone knew he had an artificial leg! Kept it a big secret during his entire career. Burt Lahr—I played his wife in "Always Leave 'Em Laughing" with Milton Berle. Anthony Perkins—he was a fabulous actor but got terribly typecast as Norman Bates. Very troubled by his sexuality. Jane Fonda? I was at a party with her and never spoke to her. She was outrageous. She's fine as an actress and an exerciser however. Ted Turner, her husband. You know, I think if a man can give two billion to the United Nations, then he's up to no good. People like Turner want this to be a one-world instead of our having America the way we want it. Dennis O'Keefe played against me in "That Certain Girl." Geraldine Page. Once someone came up to me at a meeting and said "How's it going, Geraldine?" He was gassed. There's no way I could possibly have looked like Geraldine! Janis Paige. She was testing for "Colorado Territory"—she didn't get it. I did! Jack Palance—not my favorite person. Jackie Gleason. Lily Palmer, married to Rex Harrison. Pretty girl. Foreign women are just different somehow. Veronica Lake, my dear friend Joel McCrea, Hedy Lamarr. I never met Hedy, but once she got in touch with me because she'd read a quote of mine where for some reason I said "No woman looks good with her hair parted in the middle except for Hedy Lamarr!" and she thanked me for saying that. She was one of Bob Hope's leading ladies, too. Claire Trevor. Trevor Howard. Oh, what a great actress and wonderful lady. Ida Lupino. I didn't know her too well, but one time I saw her somewhere and she said to me "you don't remember where it was we first met, do you?" I told her I had forgotten and she told me, I guess, but I can't remember.

174

Gloria De Haven. She worked hard, was a good actress, but never quite made herself into a big star. Hume Cronyn and Jessica Tandy — what a pair. Best actor and actress couple there ever was. Donald Crisp — important actor. Tony Curtis — good painter and good pusher of Tony Curtis! Ellen Corby. I worked with her when she was working on one of my sets as a secretary and she decided to become an actress and did that and was a big success. Even went on to TV — I think she was in that series called "Have Gun, Will Travel" starring Richard Boone, and then wasn't she Grandma Walton on "The Waltons?" Gladys Cooper. Sean Connery was and is still terrific. Leslie Nielsen, doing well now. Made the transition to comedy from drama. Laurel and Hardy, Celeste Holme, so elegant and classy. She too believes in getting to work on time, having the lines learned and doing the work. She and I share the same work 9 and we have and had little time for those actors and actresses who didn't play by the rules. Charles Laughton was an actor I truly admired. James Coburn — amazing character actor. Lee J. Cobb, wonderful actor. Great voice. Lots of anger. Never met him. Fred Clark. Funny, good actor and great comedian with a great slow burn! He was in "White Heat" with me. My dear Joan Caulfield. Jeff Chandler, a real he-man and played every role well. Horribly, he was operated on for a back problem and they killed him. Sterling Hayden was kind of hard to categorize. Deep voice. A real rebel. Went around the world with his kids on a sailboat. An early hippie. Harry Carey was wonderful too. Warren Beatty — did he ever do anything other than to romance ladies? Well, finally he's settled down, and I think he and his wife Annette Benning have four children now. But he wants to run for president?? Oh please. Really now. Leslie Caron. Judy Canova — I was in a play with her — "No No Nanette." Billie Burke. Yul Brenner — forceful. George Brent was in "Out of the Blue" with me. He was trying to become a comedian but I don't think he ever did. Laurel and Hardy were great comedians and really gave a lot of fun to all people who got to see their movies, and of course Charles Laughton — there was never anyone like him, nor will there be. A truly tormented man, gay, married Elsa Lanchester and never told her of his "problem" when they married, (which unfortunately was a problem back then — still is for a lot of people) but she stayed married to him anyway and they made some great films both together and separately. Ingrid Bergman. Oh, that silly, stupid so-called "scandal" about her being pregnant before she was married to that Italian director. Farrah Fawcett — I think as an actress she can behave idiotically. Rip Torn. Eddie Bracken was so darling when I worked with him in "The Girl from Jones Beach." He was just so good in that! Sylvia Sidney — boy, she's been around since the silents, hasn't she? Katharine Hepburn. She's good but you know, she really ought to quit while she's ahead! Basil Rathbone was a real king around Hollywood in his prime. I wish I'd known him. Shirley

Booth—she was wonderful. I know Ernest Borgnine slightly and knew Lloyd Bridges also. The Marx Brothers? Well, I used to see Groucho in Nate and Al's, that famous Deli in Beverly Hills. (Remember I told you that Mike used to take Mary there when she was a little girl?) Anyway, Groucho and I didn't have an opportunity to speak to one another, but he kind of stared at me. A lot. I didn't meet his brothers. Gigi Perreau was my daughter in Barefoot in the Park. Sweet kid. Weren't The Little Rascals cute? Kirk Douglas—good actor. He was very pushy though. Perry Como—I was on his radio show a lot. Fifteen minutes every day. We just talked, as I recall, because I can't sing! William Bendix was OK. Ralph Bellamy. Ed Begley was Mike's best friend, so we knew him well, but I do think his acting was a bit over-rated. Ann Baxter was a sort of friend and a very good actress. Angela Lansbury is just so very nice. Lucky to have all the success she's had. Very talented. Tallulah Bankhead was such a character. So funny and what a mouth on her! Dustin Hoffman. Red Buttons is an old favorite. Lizabeth Scott. Mary Astor. Humphrey Bogart. Peter Lawford. Elizabeth Taylor. Lauren Bacall is wonderful too. Shirley Temple. Piper Laurie—now she has staying power! She's still acting and goes from serious drama to light comedy and does it beautifully. I saw her at a party too, and she came straight up to me and we talked. And I have to confess a sense of jealousy that she's been able to keep on acting straight through her youthful years into her elderly years. But then I think there may have been certain reasons that I didn't get any more acting jobs and I'm not at all convinced that it was because I'd aged.

I've reread all of the above, and worry that it reads as nothing more than a long list of name-dropping and I guess it is. I hate to name-drop and I hate it when people name-drop around me, but I wanted you to know. Over the years people have asked and asked me if I know so and so. If I've met so and so. What's he/she like? Tell me something about him or her. And so I decided to just talk a little about some of the folks I've met along the way in this strange, crazy business I'm in. I hope it didn't bore you and that you recognized at least some of the people I mentioned! Many are from the so-called Silver Screen years, or the Golden Years of Hollywood, a thing of the past now, and I hope you'll remember those people who contributed so much to that era. I know I've left so many out and I'm sorry about that, but I just can't remember them all. But I do and I will. They say that we are all teachers and that everyone is our teacher. Thus, I've been taught by the very best and I hope I've helped some people along the way too.

I hate to come across as a whiner, but speaking of "that era," I guess I wonder about how things are going today in the business I love so. I keep reading all the time about how people are "discovered" and are just plunked into a movie. Perhaps the theory is that we all have acting talent and all we have to do it just get into a movie and we're all set. Back in my day (and I hate that phrase too!) but back in my day, people had to work and work very, very hard to get into movies. You had to pass tests. You had to be approved by everyone making that movie before you were accepted. You had to have credentials, to pay your dues as they say. Today it seems easier. If a person "looks" the part, he's given the part. It doesn't seem fair or wise, but times do change and I know that, but I feel as if the substance and grit of show business is sort of sliding off into big business deals and a lot of young sort of non-actors getting plum roles. Of course many of these people picked from obscurity do in fact become good actors. Oh I don't know. Maybe I'm just being jealous because I, as did all my contemporaries, had to put in so many years of hard work before we "made" it. So it goes, so it goes.

Would I like to work again? I think I would. But I don't know if I'm up to having all those photographs made of me showing how I look now. I don't know if I could stand all the hoopla that goes with getting back on the boards or back in films. I'm active now, I have a great life. I'm a self-taught oil painter and my paintings hang in my home and always elicit a lot compliments. If I do say so myself, and I do, I'm pretty good. I did an oil of Mike from a photograph and it looks exactly like him. He's grinning straight at the viewer, straight out at me, wearing cowboy clothes and he looks as if he's about to speak. I've done a Madonna and Child and a few still-lifes and landscapes and sometimes when I gaze at my paintings I think I could have perhaps gone that route, become an artist. But I didn't. I chose to Play Show and I did it happily and I did it well.

I frequently still attend a lot of parties where there are many celebrities and I'm always welcomed. I get to dress up in my gowns and put on the make-up again. I don't have my hair done up in a modern way any longer--—I keep it fairly long now and pull it back into a soft bun at the back of my head for special occasions and I think it looks beautiful. Today I am escorted to all my Hollywood affairs by MTV and film star Randal Malone who is my dear friend of years. He is outrageous and makes me laugh.

But aside from seeing friends and calling them, I sometimes yearn a little for the old days. After all, I made over fifty films and can't even count the plays I appeared in, many so famous; "Hello, Dolly" and "No No Nanette" and "Barefoot in the Park" and "Forty Carats." I'd love to try commercials. They are in fact a very good part of the Television scene today. I mean imagine, getting an entire story into the minds of the public in just thirty or sixty seconds. I sometimes think commercials are some of the best things on TV.

I guess my agent isn't very encouraging. But at the risk of sounding as if I have an overdeveloped ego, I have to say that when I look into the mirror I still see a beautiful woman. My hair is pure white and my skin is not very wrinkled. It's kept its pearly look. (Thank you, Mother!) I see Virginia Mayo looking back at me in the mirror and my eyes are still good so I'm not seeing myself through a thick fog! I'll admit that I can't move around as quickly as I used to, but I do move around. I think I'd do very well if I went back to work. But then, at what price?

They say that "age is just a number," and I guess I think that way too. I'm able to move around today with relative ease. I've had to have a hip replacement and I've had other operations; my appendix for example.

Of course, there's not much point in obsessing about my going back to work or anything else for that matter. If something comes up and the fates think I'm supposed to be a part of it, well then I shall! I do believe strongly that everything happens for a reason. I believe in and trust in God. Sometimes I guess it's not for us to know the reasons for why things happen in our lives. They just do. I have faith in God and He's done pretty darned well by me up to now!

CHAPTER 45

I have so many wonderful memories, memories that most people will never have. Imagine, the places I've gone and the people I've met. I sometimes wonder why it is I've been given so much. I will never understand it, but I will always be thankful and grateful for having the privileges I've been given. I've so loved my life. I have much more of it to live and I look forward to every single day of it.

When I was a little girl and used to go outside with my chums and we'd all decide what to do that day, remember? I'd be the one yelling "Let's play show!" and I'd make everybody do it. Everybody would be assigned a "role" and I'd organize the show, and we'd put it on. Would there be an audience? If we could find one, but it didn't matter. The show was the thing. It was then, it is now.

And so this is how it's been with my life. I've played show, just as I did when I was a young girl with my playmates, and I have been blessed to be able to do that for all of the best years of my life. I thank God for the gifts He's bestowed on me. I thank my audiences for letting me perform for them and for telling me so often how much they enjoyed what I did. I am grateful for all the marvelous things that have come my way. It has been the most amazing of lives, fabulous and magical. But, if you asked me to narrow it down to what I most enjoyed about my life, I'd have to say with all modesty and honesty that what I have most enjoyed was myself!

~ ~

Filmography

* The Man Next Door" (1997) .... Lucia
*L.A. Confidential" (1997) (archive footage) (uncredited) .... Herself
*Evil Spirits" (1990) .... Janet Wilson
*Santa Barbara" (1984) TV Series .... Peaches DeLight (1984)
*Fade to Black" (1980) (uncredited) .... Footage from 'White Heat'
*The Haunted" (1979) Michelle
*French Quarter" (1977) .... Countess Piazza/Ida
*Won Ton Ton, the Dog Who Saved Hollywood" (1976) Miss Batley
*Fugitive Lovers" (1975)
*Fort Utah" (1967) Linda Lee
*Castle of Evil" (1966) Mary Theresa 'Sable' Pulaski
*Young Fury" (1965) Sarah McCoy
* La Rivolta dei mercenari" (1960) Duchess de Revalte
*Jet Over the Atlantic (1959) Jean Gurney
*Westbound" (1958) Norma Putnam
*Fort Dobbs" (1958) Celia Gray
* The Tall Stranger" (1957) Ellen
*The Story of Mankind" (1957) Cleopatra
*The Big Land" (1957) Helen Jagger
*Congo Crossing" (1956) Louise Whitman
* The Proud Ones" (1956) Sally
*Great Day in the Morning" (1956) Ann Alaine
*Pearl of the South Pacific" (1955) Rita Delaine
* The Silver Chalice" (1954) Helena
*King Richard and the Crusaders" (1954) Lady Edith
*Devil's Canyon" (1953) Abby Nixon
*She's Back on Broadway" (1953) Catherine Terris
*South Sea Woman" (1953) Ginger Martin
*The Iron Mistress" (1952) Judalon de Bornay
*She's Working Her Way Through College" (1952) Angela
                Gardner/"Hot Garters Gertie"
*Painting the Clouds with Sunshine" (1951) Carol
*Starlift" (1951) Cameo appearance
*Captain Horatio Hornblower" (1951) Lady Barbara Wellesley
*Along the Great Divide" (1951) Ann Keith
*The West Point Story" (1950) Eve Dillon
*The Flame and the Arrow" (1950) Anne

*Backfire" (1950) Julie Benson
*Always Leave Them Laughing" (1949) Nancy Eagan
*Flaxy Martin" (1949) Flaxy Martin
*Red Light" (1949) Carla North
*White Heat" (1949) Verna Jarrett
*The Girl from Jones Beach" (1949) Ruth Wilson
*Colorado Territory" (1949) Colorado Carson
*Smart Girls Don't Talk" (1948) Linda Vickers
*A Song Is Born" (1948) .... Honey Swanson
*Out of the Blue (1947) Deborah Tyler
*The Secret Life of Walter Mitty" (1947) Rosalind van Hoorn
*The Best Years of Our Lives"(1946) Marie Derry
*The Kid from Brooklyn" (1946) Polly Pringle
*Wonder Man" (1945) Ellen Shavley
*Seven Days Ashore" (1944) Carol Dean
*The Princess and the Pirate" (1944) Princess Margaret
*Up in Arms" (1944) (as The Goldwyn Girls) Goldwyn" Girl
*Jack London" (1943) Mamie
*Follies Girl" (1943)

Photo Credits:

We are indebted to AOL Time-Warner and MGM Studios for permission to use film stills with copyrights as noted below. Professional photos in later years provided by Michael W. Schwibs, Hollywood Photographer, 929 Rutland Ave, Los Angeles, CA 90042. Many of the photos are family snapshots or publicity photos from the private collection of Virginia Mayo. We have done our best to identify the sources and ownerships of all photos. Please let us know of any errors or omissions and they will be corrected

"Jack London" — 1944. MGM
"Princess & the Pirate" — 1944, MGM.
"The Best Years of our Lives" — 1946 MGM.
"The Secret Life of Walter Mitty" — 1946 MGM.
"The Girl from Jones Beach" — 1949 Turner Entertainment Co.
        All Rights Reserved (WB)
"White Heat"- 1949 Turner Entertainment Co. All Rights Reserved (WB)
"The Flame & the Arrow" — 1950 Norma F.R. Productions Inc. (WB)
"The Iron Mistress" — 1952 Warner Bros. All Rights Reserved
"South Sea Woman" — 1953 Warner Bros. All Rights reserved
"The Silver Chalice"--1954 Victor Saville Productions. All Rights
        Reserved (WB)
"She's Working Her Way Through College" — 1952 Warner Bros.
        All Rights Reserved.
"Colorado Territory." — 1949 Turner Entertainment Co. All Rights
        reserved (WB)
"The West Point Story." — 1950 Warner Bros. All Rights Reserved
"Captain Horatio Hornblower" — 1950 Warner Bros. All Rights Reserved
"King Richard and the Crusaders" 1954 Warner Bros. All Rights Reserved
"She's Back on Broadway" — 1953 Warner Bros. All Rights Reserved
"The Kid from Brooklyn" — 1946 MGM
Photos by Michael W. Schwibs — Michael W. Schwibs
"Along the Great Divide" — 1951 Warner Bros. All Rights Reserved
"Devils Canyon" — 1953 RKO Pictures Inc. All Rights Reserved
"Seven Days Ashore" — 1944 RKO Pictures Inc. All Rights Reserved
"Always Leave Them Laughing" — 1949 Turner Entertainment Co
        All Rights Reserved (WB)
The drawing of Virginia Mayo used on the cover is by David Fairrington,
— David Fairrington, fine art & portraiture, 310-618-8603
fairrington@mindspring.com,
http://fairrington.home.mindspring.com

Index

A

Adams, Edie 3, 168
Albert, Eddie 172
Allyson, June ... 28, 58, 59, 102,
   157, 166
Ameche, Don 172
Andrews Sisters ... 18, 152, 172
Andrews, Dana 44, 77, 113, 168
Andrews, Maxine 131, 152
Angeli., Pier 170
Ann-Margret 168
Arden, Eve 44, 172
Arnold, Edward 168
Astaire, Fred 56, 57, 166
Astor, Mary 176

B

Bacall, Lauren 176
Ball, Lucille 168
Bankhead, Tallulah 176
Barrymore, Drew 170
Barrymore, John 92, 170
Barrymore, Lionel 44, 170
Baxter, Ann 176
Beatty, Warren 175
Beery, Wallace 167
Begley, Ed 176
Behan, Brendan 121
Belinda, Johnny 170
Bellamy, Ralph 166, 176
Bendix, William 176

Bennett, Tony 169
Benning, Annette 175
Bergman, Ingrid 38, 160, 175
Berle, Milton 55, 84, 174
Berlin, Irving 169
Bishop, Bill 130
Black, Karen 154
Blyth, Ann 60
Bogart, Humphrey 176
Bolger, Ray 168
Bond, Ward 60
Boone, Richard 175
Booth, Shirley 176
Borgnine, Ernest 176
Botticher, Bud 108
Boyer, Charles 142, 160
Boyle, Johnny 83
Bracken, Eddie 175
Brando, Marlon 90
Brennan, Walter 85, 170
Brenner, Yul 175
Brent, George 175
Bridges, Lloyd 176
Bronson, Charles 59
Brosnan, Pierce 159
Burke, Billie 169, 175
Burke, Katherine 14
Burton, Richard 170
Buttons, Red 176

C

Caesar, Sid 38

Cagney, Jimmy.. 43, 49, 76, 77, 83, 107
Cahn, Sammy...................... 83
Callan, Mickey 138
Canova, Judy 175
Cantor, Eddie 20, 21, 47
Carey, Harry 175
Carmichael, Hoagie...... 44, 172
Caron, Leslie 175
Carson, Jack 167
Casavettes, John............... 174
Caulfield, Joan..... 65, 144, 152, 154, 175
Chandler, Jeff.............. 44, 175
Chaney, Lon 172
Charisse, Cyd..................... 56
Charisse, Nico 77
Christie, Audrey................... 10
Clark, Dane 79
Clark, Fred......................... 175
Cobb, Lee J. 175
Coburn, Charles 174
Coburn, James 175
Cochran, Steve... 43, 44, 46, 93
Cohen, Mickey........... 126, 127
Coleman, Ronald............... 167
Como, Perry 176
Connery, Sean 175
Connors, Chuck................... 66
Conway, Tom 87
Cooper, Gary.......... 41, 65, 170
Cooper, Gladys 175
Cooper, Jackie 174
Corby, Ellen....................... 175
Corey, Wendell.................. 169
Crain, Jeannie 170
Crawford, Broderick.... 169, 170
Crawford, Joan............. 60, 167
Crisp, Donald..................... 175
Cronyn, Hume 175
Crosby, Bing....................... 73
Crumbaker, Marge 131

Cukor, George..................... 34
Cummings, Robert 170
Curtis, Tony 50, 175

D

Dailey, Dan....................... 170
Damone, Vic...................... 169
Darnell, Linda 173
Davis, Bette 59, 60, 61, 65, 167
Day, Dennis........................ 60
Day, Doris 83, 169
Day, Laraine...................... 166
De Carlo, Yvonne 170
de Fore, Don 92
De Haven, Gloria............... 175
de Havilland, Olivia............ 170
De Mille, Cecil B. 135
Dean, James 88, 168
Diamond, Frances 38
Dietrich, Marlena 168
Dillon,Cliff 6
Dorsey,Jimmy...................... 17
Dougherty, Jim .. 48, 51, 95, 99, 170
Douglas, Kirk 85, 176
Douglas, Mike.................... 159
Dowling, Connie 33
Duggan, Andrew............... 167
Dunleavy, Brian................. 169
Dunne, Irene...................... 170
Dunne, Jimmy 130
Duvall, Robert.................... 171

E

Eddington, Nora 92
Ellen, Vera. 44, See , See , See , See
Enright, Florence............ 77, 98
Evans, Dale........................ 173

F

Fawcett, Farrah 175
Faye, Alice........................... 172
Fitzgerald, Barry 173
FitzGerald, Ella.................... 16
Fleming, Rhonda 37, 99, 166
Flynn, Errol 92, 93, 170, 172
Foch, Nina 173
Fonda, Henry...................... 168
Fonda, Jane 142, 174
Fontaine, Joan.................... 173
Fontane Margot 56
Ford, Glenn 174
Fosse, Bob 174
Foy, Eddy 97
Francis, Kay 174

G

Gable,Clark 2, 34, 80
Gabor, Eva 174
Gabor, Magda 174
Gabor, Zsa Zsa 169, 174
Garbo, Greta 172, 173
Garfield, John 174
Garland, Judy 21, 73, 74, 95
Garrett, Betty 173
Gay,Marguerite.................. 3, 5
Gershwin, George 169
Gleason, Jackie.................. 174
Goldwyn, Sam1, 24, 25, 26, 27,
    28, 29, 31, 32, 33, 34, 35,
    37, 38, 41, 43, 44, 45, 47,
    49, 76, 77, 80, 108, 170, 182
Goodman, Benny 17
Grable, Betty 28, 80, 141
Graham, Lee 171
Grahame, Gloria................. 173
Granger, Farley 173
Granger, Stewart 170
Grant, Cary.......... 20, 102, 169

Gray, Glen........................... 17
Grayson, Kathryn 166, 173
Griffin, Merv.............. 160, 174

H

Hale, Alan........................... 83
Haley, Jack........................ 168
Hamilton, George 171
Hardy, Oliver 175
Harris, Phil......................... 172
Harrison, Rex 68, 95, 174
Harvey, Laurence 96
Hawn, Goldie....................... 59
Hayden, Sterling................ 175
Haymes, Dick 170
Hayworth, Rita............ 28, 170
Heflin, Van......................... 169
Henried, Paul..................... 173
Hepburn, Audrey 173
Hepburn, Katharine 20, 173,
    175
Heston, Charlton 167, 168
Hoffman, Dustin................. 176
Holme, Celeste.................. 175
Hope, Bob .. 3, 31, 81, 160, 174
Hope, Delores 172
Howard, Trevor................... 174
Hudson, Rock................ 53, 88
Hughes, Howard 96, 97, 98, 99,
    113, 169, 170
Hunter, Jeffrey................... 103
Hunter, Tab 167
Huston, John 44, 77, 113

J

Jeffreys, Anne 166
Jergens, Adele 47
Johnson, Van 151, 152, 172
Jolson, Al........................... 173
Jones, Jack 169

Jones,Lea.... 3, 4, 7, 10, 11, 75, 139

K

Kahn, Sammy..................... 169
Karloff, Boris....................... 168
Kaye, Danny 32, 33, 37, 38, 39, 45, 46, 47, 172
Kaye, Sylvia.......................... 38
Keith, Brian....................... 173
Kelly, Gene.......................... 56
Kelly, Grace.......................... 73
Kennedy, John Fitzgerald... 120
Kerr, Deborah..................... 170
Keyes, Evelyn..................... 166
King, Eleanor........................ 26
Kirshbaum, Audrey.............. 47
Korda, Alex........................ 174
Kovacs, Ernie 3, 168

L

Ladd, Alan 63, 64, 107
Lake, Veronica 174
Lamarr, Hedy........ 28, 108, 174
Lamas, Fernando 173
Lamour, Dorothy.. 28, 159, 172, 173
Lancaster, Burt . 59, 66, 80, 105
Lanchester, Elsa................. 175
Landis, Carole 28, 45
Lansbury, Angela 160, 176
Laughton, Charles.............. 175
Laurel, Stan........................ 175
Laurie, Piper 176
Lawford, Peter 170, 176
Lee, Anna........................... 109
Leigh, Janet....................... 166
Leigh, Vivien................. 82, 170
Lewis, Jerry 167
Lindbergh,Charles 8, 9

Lindfors, Viveca................... 79
Lindsay, Margaret.............. 166
Loren, Sophia..................... 169
Lorre, Peter 61, 102, 167
Lovejoy, Frank.................... 167
Loy, Myrna 44, 168
Lupino, Ida 174
Lynfors, Vivaca.................. 167
Lynn, Diana 167

M

Mac Laine, Shirley............. 167
MacRae Gordon..... 79, 83, 174
Madison, Guy 108, 166, 169
Malden, Karl 167
Mann, Ted 99
Mansfield, Jayne 168
March, Frederick 44, 168
Marcos, Imelda................... 171
Marshall, Herbert............... 174
Martin, Tony 170
Marx Brothers..................... 176
Marx, Groucho................... 108
Mason, James............... 73, 95
Massey, Ilona 109
Massey, Raymond.............. 167
Matthau, Walter................... 59
Maxwell, Marilyn................ 167
Mayo, Andrew 14, 16
McCambridge, Mercedes ... 173
McCarthy, Senator Joseph 104, 105, 173
McCormack, Patty.............. 142
McCrea, Joel 174
McCreedy, George 109
McGuire, Dorothy . 85, 166, 170
McQueen, Steve................. 169
McRea, Joel 103, 166
Menjou, Adolph 167
Merman, Ethel.................... 167
Merrill, Dina 172

Miller, Ann 28, 157, 168
Miller, Glenn 17
Mills, John 64, 168
Mineo, Sal 168
Miranda, Carmen................. 47
Mitchell, Betty 131
Mitchum, Robert 168
Monroe, Marilyn 51, 95, 99, 170
Montalban, Ricardo 102
Morgan, Dennis 37, 86, 87
Morocco, Sultan of . 2, 100, 135
Mullaney, Jack.................... 142
Muny, Municipal Opera .6, 1, 9,
    10, 13, 14, 16, 86, 103, 137,
    169
Murphy, Audie 168

N

Nader, George.................... 102
Natwick, Mildred 168
Neal, Patricia 42, 64, 173
Nelson, Gene 56, 83, 86, 91,
    173
Nelson, Ozzie 15
Nelson,Harriet Hilliard .. 15, 166
Newman, Paul 95, 100, 101,
    103
Nielsen, Leslie 175
Nolan, Lloyd 160, 173
Novak, Kim......................... 174
Nureyev, Rudolf................... 56

O

Oberon, Merle 24, 174
O'Brien, Edmund 79, 107
O'Brien, Margaret .. 59, 74, 142,
    157, 168
O'Brien, Pat....................... 168
O'Donnell................ 44, 47, 168
O'Hara, Maureen 173

O'Keefe, Dennis 138, 174
Olivier, Laurence 24
Olsen, Dale 171
O'Shea, Michael .. 3, 30, 37, 41,
    42, 46, 52, 118, 126, 127,
    147, 151

P

Page, Geraldine 174
Paige, Janis....................... 174
Palance, Jack............ 101, 174
Palmer, Lily........................ 174
Pansy the Horse 14, 15, 16, 17,
    18, 20, 23, 38, 118, 137
Parks, Larry 173
Pate, Michael..................... 102
Peck, Gregory 34, 85, 170
Peppard, George................. 63
Perkins, Anthony 174
Perreau, Gigi 142, 176
Peters, Jean 169
Pigeon, Walter............. 96, 170
Pitts, Zazu 169
Pleshette Suzanne 169
Pope John 110
Porter, Cole 169
Powell, Eleanor 169
Powell, Jane 28, 102, 168
Powell, William 174
Power, Tyrone 173
Presley, Elvis..................... 169
Price, Vincent 168
Prowse, Juliet.................... 57

Q

Quinn, Anthony................... 172

R

Radio City Music Hall 9, 14, 20, 22
Raft, George......... 76, 109, 167
Rains, Claude...................... 61
Rand, Ayn........................... 42
Randall, Tony 169
Rathbone, Basil................. 175
Raye, Martha..................... 168
Reagan, Ronald ... 92, 167, 170
Redford, Robert.. 102, 142, 170
Reisman, Leo 17
Remick, Lee 170
Rennie, Michael.................. 170
Reynolds, Burt.................... 169
Reynolds, Debbie 170
Ritter, Thelma.................... 167
Robards, Jason 172
Robertson, Cliff.................. 172
Robertson, Dale 113
Robinson, Edward G. 172
Rockettes 20
Rockwell, Norman 173
Rogers, Ginger 28, 166
Rogers, Roy 173
Roland, Gilbert 170
Rolands, Gena 174
Roman, Ruth 101, 174
Romero, Caesar................. 172
Rooney, Mickey........... 95, 169
Rose, Billy 22, 23, 24, 25, 38
Roselli, John...................... 130
Russell, Harold.................... 44
Russell, Jane.......... 98, 99, 166
Russell, Rosalind.......... 70, 169
Rutherford, Ann.................. 173
Ryan, Robert 102

S

Salt, Waldo 105

Sanders, George..... 87, 95, 96, 169
Schriber, Elsa.................... 100
Scott, Lizabeth........... 166, 176
Scott, Randolph.......... 108, 167
Scott, Zachary 169
Selleck, Tom...................... 169
Selznick, David O. 25
Sharaff, Irene...................... 47
Shaw, Artie.................. 17, 166
Shearer, Norma.................. 167
Sheen, Bishop Fulton 88
Sheridan, Ann.................... 169
Sherman, Vincent................ 79
Shore, Dinah 17, 18, 33, 159
Sidney, Sylvia.................... 175
Simmons, Jean.................. 174
Sinatra, Frank.................... 169
Skelton, Red...................... 169
Slezak, Walter 138
Smith, Alexis.............. 171, 174
Sothern, Ann 169
Spelling, Aaron.................. 160
Stack, Robert..................... 101
Stanwyck, Barbara 170
Steiger, Rod 169
Sterling, Jan 170
Stewart, Jimmy....... 20, 58, 174
Strasberg, Susan................ 166
Styne, Jules......................... 83
Sullavan, Margaret 170
Susanne, Jacqueline............ 21

T

Talbot, Lyle....................... 142
Tandy, Jessica 175
Taylor, Elizabeth........... 88, 176
Taylor, Robert..... 105, 171, 174
Temple, Shirley 167, 176
Tierney, Gene.................... 170
Tone, Franchot................... 170

Torme, Mel 148, 149, 169
Torn, Rip............................ 175
Tracy, Spencer 92, 173
Trevor, Claire..................... 174
Turner, Lana........................ 28
Turner, Ted........................ 174

V

Vallee, Rudy 166
Van Doren, Mamie 168
Villechaize, Herve.............. 102

W

Wagner, Robert 170
Walker, Clint 108
Walker, Robert 170, 173
Walsh, Raoul 53, 76
Ward, Amelita...................... 29
Warner Brothers 43, 45, 53, 79,
    80, 82, 83, 87, 100, 103,
    108, 167
Warner, Jack 34, 35, 91
Washington,George . 2, 89, 144

Wayne, John 167, 169
Webb, Clifton..................... 170
Weismueller, Johnny 168
Wells, Orson...................... 170
West, Mae 27, 28, 76, 167
Widmark, Richard.............. 168
Wilde, Cornel..................... 170
Williams, Esther... 28, 157, 158,
    173
Winters, Shelley 169
Withers, Jane 170
Wright, Teresa........ 44, 77, 168
Wyatt, Jane 166
Wyler, Willie......................... 77
Wyman, Jane 170
Wymore, Pat................... 92, 93
Wymore, Patrice................. 92
Wynn, Ed........................... 168
Wynn, Keenan.................... 168

Y

Young, Loretta................... 169
Young, Roland................... 170

With brother Lea
in St. Louis, 1921.

With brother Lea in
St. Louis, ca. 1924.

Father Luke, Lea and me on
Arlington Street, Saint
Louis, 1923.

My mother, Lea and
me at "The Big River."

Muny Opera girls. I'm
the one in the middle.

Marguerite Gay and I
doing a number called "I
Like Mountain Music."

My partner in a skit called "Stars
are the Windows of Heaven."

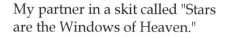

A Postcard from my daddy commemorating
the Spirit of Saint Louis.

A riotous offering wherein "Pansy" is depicted by two men in a horse skin, directed by a very glamorous young lady who is truly a 'symphony for the eyes' ... so beautiful is her face and figure. She was the winner of "The Perfect Legs Contest." This is a comedy offering throughout; "Pansy" being the favorite entry in the 'Laugh Derby'!

FERDINAND, THE BULL
made his debut at the Radio City Music Hall

FOUR (4) WEEKS ENGAGEMENT
Jan. 1st to Jan. 28th, 1941
ANDY MAYO & CO.
presents
"FERDINAND"

Here's the Vaudeville show that ending up branding me as a "Mayo" girl.

194

Everone has to work with one sometime.

PANSY IS A PANIC!

say the critics

★ "That horse in the show shops named 'Pansy' and walks like a sissy, makes the sides ache too much . . ."
—*Walter Winchell*

★ "One of the most unusual acts ever seen in a cafe. An innovation that everyone should see."
—*"Speed" Kendall, Times*

★ "Our idea of one of the funniest night club acts in ages is 'Pansy' the performing horse at the Biltmore."
—*Harrison Carroll, Herald-Express*

★ "A. Mayo presents Pansy, the Wonder Horse. The animal, cleverest horse that has ever walked across a stage, is good for a lot of laughs."
—*Philadelphia Record*

★ "Pansy, the Horse, is our candidate for the best feature of the week. Completely nonchalant and thoroughly imbued with j' nai sas pas, Pansy trots off with all honors on the Earle's stage and gives the feature picture a run for the money. A trained horse, a thoroughbred and a comedian. Pansy deserves all the bows the audience can, and probably will, accord her."
—*Washington Press*

★ "Rudy Vallee, in his engagement at the Astor Roof, must share billing with a horse named Pansy . . ."
—*Danton Walker*

Phone . . . Wire
or Write . . .
**AVAILABLE
FOR DATES**

Personal Management of EDWARD E. SMITH
22 W. 48th Street • New York City
PHONE: BRYANT 9-0543

ANDY MAYO presents

Pansy the Horse

Sam Goldwyn greeting me on
my first day at the studio.

An early glamour photo.

On the set of "Jack London" with my future
husband, Michael O'Shea. ©1944. MGM

With Mother, Martha, on our way to New York.

With Mother, Martha and dog, "Dinky."

"Princess & the Pirate" with Bob Hope ©1944, MGM.

With Dana Andrews, from "The Best Years of our Lives."
©1946 MGM.

My beloved Aunt Alice in my dressing room at the studio
while filming "Best Years."

With Danny Kaye in a scene from "The Secret Life of Walter Mitty"
©1946 MGM.

Fun with Ronald Reagan on the Beach while
filming "The Girl from Jones Beach," 1946

A scene from "The Girl from Jones Beach."
©1949 Turner Entertainment Co. All Rights Reserved (WB)

Tough guy James Cagney in a scene from "White Heat."
©1949 Turner Entertainment Co. All Rights Reserved (WB)

With Burt Lancaster in "The Flame & the Arrow."
©1950 Norma F.R. Productions Inc. (WB)

With Alan Ladd in a scene from "The Iron Mistress."

With Burt Lancaster—dressed to kill—
in a scene from "South Seas Woman."

With Paul Newman in "The Silver Chalice," not exactly his favorite movie.
©1954 Victor Saville Productions. All Rights Reserved (WB)

"She'sWorking Her Way Through College."

At the Hollywood premiere of "King Richard and the Crusaders" with Jack Warner.

With Elizabeth Taylor and Michael Wilding at a fabulous Hollywood premiere.

In the presence of the great artist Norman Rockwell.

With Gregory Peck in "Captain Horatio Hornblower."

Royal command performance in England. English actor
John Mills, Michael O'Shea and me meeting Prince Philip.

The land of enchantment where we filmed "Colorado Territory."

With Rex Harrison in "King Richard and the Crusaders."
©1954 Warner Bros. All Rights Reserved

With Danny Kaye in "The Kid from Brooklyn."
© 1946 MGM

216

"She's Back on Broadway."

Cheesecake.

Sweater girl photo.

Another publicity photo.

Publicity Photos.

218

"West Point Story." Alan Hale Jr., Gene Nelson, Me, Jimmy Cagney, Doris Day and Gordon MacRae. ©1950 Warner Bros. All Rights Reserved

My wedding day, wearing an
Irene Sharaff original, July 6, 1947.

Newlywed Holidays.

Together at the ranch.

Our dogs, Annie and
Patrick, in the corral.

With Mary Catherine in 1953,
my toughest role yet!

With grandmother, Martha Jones,
and Mary in her christening clothes.

With Mary and proud
Dad, Michael, at home.

On the set of "The Tall Stranger" on
location in Thousand Oaks California.

Outdoor fun, or is it?

Playing around at home in Van Nuys.

The family home in Thousand Oaks in the '60s. Can you tell?

Quality time with Mary Catherine.

Still staying on my toes.

Another publicity shot.

With Judy Garland, Patty McCormack and Jack Mullaney in the Spring of 1969. Judy died several weeks later. Photo by Michael W. Schwibs.

I remain active, attending many Hollywood parties and social events. Here, I'm with other famous glamour queens of the silver screen: child star Jane Withers, legendary Oscar-winning Margaret O'Brien, MGM's top tapper Ann Miller, film star Randal Malone and the beautiful Rhonda Fleming. Photo by Michael W. Schwibs.

In December of 2000, I was the recipient of the Lifetime Achievement Award
from the Southern California Motion Picture Council. Presenting the award
to me are two of my dearest friends, Margaret O'Brien and Randal Malone.
In my acceptance speech I said, "I'm very honored and grateful. This is one
of the happiest moments of my life."
Photo by Michael W. Schwibs.

Portrait during my most active years in Hollywood.

A later portrait.

A treasured painting by David Fairrington.

Books by LC VanSavage

*To Norma Jeane With Love, Jimmie -Jim Dougherty as told to LC Van Savage (2001) ISBN 1-888725-51-6 The sensitive and touching story of Jim Dougherty's teenage bride who later became Marilyn Monroe. Dozens of photographs. "The Marilyn Monroe book of the year!" As seen on TV. 5½X8½, 200 pp, $16.95

*Virginia Mayo—The Best Years of My Life (2002) Autobiography of film star Virginia Mayo as told to LC Van Savage. From her early days in Vaudeville and the Muny in St Louis to the dozens of hit motion pictures, with dozens of photographs. ISBN 1-888725-53-2, 7 X 10, 220 pp, $18.95

Order form			
Item	Each	Quantity	Amount
Missouri (only) sales tax 7.425%			
Priority Shipping			$5.00
	Total		
Ship to Name:			
Address:			
City State Zip:			

BeachHouse
Books

www.beachhousebooks.com

BeachHouse Books
PO Box 7151
 Chesterfield, MO 63006-7151
(636) 394-4950
Beachhouse books.com

230

Made in United States
Orlando, FL
13 July 2022

19709661R00130